Fortress • 2

Hadrian's Wall
AD 122–410

Nic Fields • Illustrated by D Spedaliere & S Sulemsohn Spedaliere

Series editors Marcus Cowper and Nikolai Bogdanovic

First published in Great Britain in 2003 by Osprey Publishing, Elms Court, Chapel Way, Botley, Oxford OX2 9LP, United Kingdom.
Email: info@ospreypublishing.com

ISBN 1 84176 430 2

Editorial: Ilios Publishing, Oxford, UK (www.iliospublishing.com)
Design: Ken Vail Graphic Design, Cambridge, UK
Index by Alison Worthington
Originated by Grasmere Digital Imaging, Leeds, UK
Printed and bound by L-Rex Printing Company Ltd.

03 04 05 06 07   10 9 8 7 6 5 4 3 2 1

A CIP catalogue record for this book is available from the British Library.

FOR A CATALOGUE OF ALL BOOKS PUBLISHED BY OSPREY MILITARY AND AVIATION PLEASE CONTACT:

Osprey Direct USA, c/o MBI Publishing, PO Box 1,
729 Prospect Ave, Osceola, WI 54020, USA.
Email: info@ospreydirectusa.com

Osprey Direct UK, PO Box 140, Wellingborough,
Northants, NN8 2FA, United Kingdom.
Email: info@ospreydirect.co.uk

www.ospreypublishing.com

Editor's note

When classical authors are referred to throughout the text the standard form of reference has been adopted. The formula used is 'author', 'title' (if the author wrote more than one work) followed by either a two- or three-figure reference, indicating 'book, 'chapter' and 'paragraph'. Thus 'Polybius (6.33–7)' refers to chapters 33 to 37 of the sixth book of the only surviving work by Polybius, whilst 'Tacitus *Annales* 13.35' refers to the 35th chapter of the 13th book of the *Annales* by Tacitus.

Artist's note

Our sincere thanks to all who have helped in the preparation of this book, especially to Marcus Cowper and Nikolai Bogdanovic who believed in us and gave us the wonderful opportunity to illustrate the book, and Dr. Nic Fields, who enabled us to go deep into the subject with his great knowledge. This book is dedicated to our dearest daughter Alina, and to our parents, Misu, Edith, Antonio and Maria.

Readers may care to note that the original paintings from which the colour plates in this book were prepared are available for private sale. All reproduction copyright whatsoever is retained by the Publishers. All enquiries should be addressed to:

Sarah Sulemsohn
Tel-Fax: 00-39-0575-692210
info@alinaillustrazioni.com
alina@alinaillustrazioni.com
www.alinaillustrazioni.com

The Publishers regret that they can enter into no correspondence upon this matter.

Abbreviations

AE	L'Année Épigraphique, Paris, 1888–
BAR	British Archaeological Reports, Oxford
BMC III	Coins of the Roman Empire in the British Museum III, London, 1936
CIL	Corpus Inscriptionum Latinarum, Berlin, 1862–
CPL	Corpus Papyrorum Latinarum, Wiesbaden, 1956–8
ILS	Inscriptiones Latinae Selectae, 2nd edition, Berlin, 1954
P. Mich	Papyri in the University of Michigan Collection, Ann Arbor, 1931–
P. Oxy.	The Oxyrhynchus Papyri, London, 1898–
RIB	Roman Inscriptions of Britain I, 2nd edition, Stroud, 1995
RMR	Roman Military Records on Papyrus, New Haven, 1971
SB	Sammelbuch griechischer Urkunden aus Ägypten, Strassburg, Leipzig, Heidelberg, Wiesbaden, 1913–
SHA	Scriptores Historiae Augustae
SP	Select Papyri: non-literary Papyri, Cambridge, Mass., 1923–4
Tab. Vindol. II	The Vindolanda Writing Tablets II, London, 1994

Contents

Introduction

As the first century AD matured, the boundaries of the Roman Empire become increasingly fixed, and what were once temporary stop lines become firm frontiers. Significantly, from the Latin for frontier, *limes* (pl. *limites*), we gain our word 'limit'. Consequently, the army's role predominately became one of policing the frontier tribes, preventing livestock rustling and tax evasion, mounting punitive raids, and showing the flag to friendly tribes outside the empire.

The frontiers of the empire took many forms. Some of them were completely open with scarcely any boundary definition, while a military road marked others. Some of them followed the lines of rivers, while others were closed off with manmade barriers. The latter were not of uniform design, except that most were accompanied by one or more ditches. Hadrian's Wall was extremely elaborate, composed of three separate defensive features, a ditch to the north, then the wide stone curtain-wall with turrets, milecastles and forts strung out along it, and finally a larger earthwork to the south. Running some 75 miles from sea to sea, it has been justifiably described as over the top. Other frontiers were less complex. In Germania, Hadrian built a palisade fronted by a ditch, replaced at a later date by a bank of earth. In Britannia Hadrian's Wall was replaced for a short time by the Antonine Wall, 45 miles to the north, built not in stone, but turf-blocks. In Raetia, approximately the area of modern Switzerland and Austria, a stone curtain-wall was constructed, but not so wide as Hadrian's Wall. In Africa stretches of dry-stone walling have been found marking sections of this very long frontier, other sections of which were left open, but not necessarily unguarded as is evident from a number of blockhouses.

In most frontier provinces legionary fortresses were situated in the interior, some distance behind the borders. On parts of the Rhine and Danube, particularly where the frontiers were marked by the rivers themselves, the legions were stationed at strategic points close to the river banks, sometimes so close that the fortresses were washed away and had to be rebuilt further back from the rivers. Auxiliary troops were generally stationed in forts on the line of the frontier itself, actually attached to them as on Hadrian's Wall and the Antonine Wall, or some short distance (*c.* 1 mile) behind them, as in Germania and Raetia. Most frontiers were equipped with smaller fortlets like the milecastles attached to Hadrian's Wall, or the freestanding *Kleinkastellen* along the Rhine. In between these were usually watchtowers.

The Wall at Walltown Crags, looking south-west from turret 45a (Walltown), showing the facing-stones and rubble-core used in its construction. This is a section of the Narrow Wall. (Author's Collection)

Roman fortifications

Most of our knowledge concerning the layout and terminology of Roman military installations derives from two literary sources. The earliest surviving description of a marching-camp is that given by Polybius (6.33–7), who was writing in the middle of the second century BC. In the reign of Trajan (AD 98–117) a surveyor commonly known as Hyginus Gromaticus wrote a theoretical surveying manual (*De munitionibus castrorum*), which was intended to provide the appropriate accommodation for every type of army unit the student was likely to encounter. Despite being written nearly three hundred years apart both accounts are still broadly comparable, with divergences due mainly to the differing needs of an army in permanent garrison as opposed to a temporary rest camp. Archaeology and aerial reconnaissance, especially in Britain, have demonstrated that the basic principles laid down by these two writers were incorporated into the planning of fortifications from the late Republic until well into the third century AD.

When the army was on campaign it constructed marching-camps to provide security at night, and, once an area was conquered, a network of turf and timber forts roughly a day's march apart. In Britannia this phase lasted until the mid-80s AD. Additionally, before the legions had established their permanent bases in Britannia, they constructed fortresses either to provide part of a legion with a summer campaign base (*castra aestiva*) or winter quarters (*castra hiberna*). Once the army was no longer poised to continue the expansion of the empire these fortresses and forts became permanent, their plan and design preserving the main defensive features of the marching-camp from which they had evolved. The shallow ditch and palisade of the latter were, however, replaced by more substantial earthworks in permanent fortifications, often with two or more V-shaped ditches and an earth or turf rampart surmounted by a timber parapet. The four gateways were retained, but towers now defended them, and further towers were added at the four angles and at intervals between.

It should be emphasised that there is no such thing as a typical Roman fortress, fort or marching-camp. The basic layout of a fortress, for instance, was

A turf and timber fort, as depicted on Trajan's Column (Scene LI), showing detail of the installation's fortified gateway and angle-towers. The two buildings just inside the fort appear to be granaries. (Reproduced from Lepper, F. and Frere, S. S., *Trajan's Column: A New Edition of the Chicorius Plates*, Sutton, Stroud, 1988)

supposed to be standardised, but closer examination shows that there were considerable differences in detail between individual fortress plans, and between the same types of building at different sites. What follows, therefore, is an outline illustrating the different categories of Roman military installations.

Fortresses

Prior to Domitian (r. AD 81–96), fortresses were permanent bases accommodating two legions. During Domitian's reign, however, fortresses were reduced in size (*c.* 20–25ha) and housed only one legion, or were smaller still (*c.* 10–15ha) and housed either a full legion or several of its cohorts, sometimes with auxiliary troops, for a campaign. The term 'vexillation fortress' was coined by archaeologists for the latter type of site.

Forts

The framework of Roman occupation and control was firmly based on the fort (*c.* 1–5ha), a permanent base accommodating an auxiliary unit. The layout of the auxiliary fort was essentially a miniature of the legionary fortress plan.

A fort of the period AD 80–125 was protected by an earth rampart – encased with either timber or turf and founded upon a bed of logs or a stone base – surmounted by a spilt-timber breastwork or wattle hurdles and fronted by one or more V-shaped ditches. The rampart was pierced by four gateways, each with a timber tower above the gate passage itself or towers to either side. Further towers, set within the body of the rampart, stood at the angles as well as being spaced at regular intervals around the perimeter. The forts along Hadrian's Wall, however, were built with curtain-walls, towers and gateways of stone.

Tacitus (b. *c.* AD 55) rightly calls the fort the 'soldiers' hearth and home' (*Historiae* 2.80), the objective being to provide a permanent and tolerably comfortable quarter for its garrison. As such, it compared well with the fortress of the legions. It also had to be secure against the possibility of surprise attack. However, a fort was not designed as an impregnable stronghold. On the contrary it was a jumping-off point, a base for wide-ranging activities. In wartime the enemy was engaged at close-quarters in the field, while at other times the garrison would have patrolled well beyond the frontier, either to support allied tribes or to conduct punitive campaigns.

Fortlets

A very much smaller installation was the fortlet (*c.* 1ha). Placed at intermediate points along a frontier system, along a road, or at a river crossing, these usually accommodated a century or more of an auxiliary cohort. A fortlet, unlike a fort, only had a single gate through the rampart, with a timber tower above, and one or two ditches beyond. With their towered gateways fortlets would have fulfilled a 'see and be seen' role.

Watchtowers

Commodus (r. AD 180–192), so as to safeguard the provincials of Mauretania Caesariensis, modern Algeria, 'built new watchtowers and repaired the old ones by the work of his soldiers' (*ILS* 396). Invariably only three or four metres square at the base and at least two storeys high, the term is often used indiscriminately, but is usually taken to cover small sites without significant barrack accommodation. Probably manned by a *contubernium* of eight men, these installations were usually made of timber, set within a low rampart and a single or double ditch, and spaced out along a road or river to observe traffic and population movement.

Marching-camps

Josephus (b. AD 37) says that whenever the Romans entered hostile territory, they would 'first construct their camp' (*Bellum Iudaicum* 3.76). Marching-camps,

LEFT A turf and timber fortlet on the Danube frontier, as depicted on Trajan's Column (Scene I), showing detail of the installation's fortified gateway and timber palisade. (Reproduced from Lepper, F. and Frere, S. S., *Trajan's Column: A New Edition of the Chicorius Plates*, Sutton, Stroud, 1988)

BELOW A watchtower on the Danube frontier constructed of turf-blocks, as depicted on Trajan's Column (Scene I), although the first-floor balcony and palisade are of timber. A torch for signalling purposes projects from the upper window. (Reproduced from Lepper, F. and Frere, S. S., *Trajan's Column: A New Edition of the Chicorius Plates*, Sutton, Stroud, 1988)

to which Josephus is referring, were overnight halts for armies or units on campaign. Each had a shallow ditch and low earth rampart constructed of material thrown up from the ditch, some 1.5 metres high, topped with a palisade made up of the two wooden stakes (*pila muralia*) carried by each soldier. Rather than having one end driven into the ground, it is now believed that the *pila muralia* were tied together in groups of three to form a kind of large 'caltrop'.

There were no gates in the gateways of a marching-camp as sentries guarded them. The open gateway would normally receive additional protection from a mound with a ditch (*titulus*), which was built several metres to its front, or through an extension of the rampart (*clavicula*) that curved either outwards or inwards. These camps provided a simple measure of security for troops camped under canvas.

Practice-camps

Sextus Iulius Frontinus, governor of Britannia (AD 73/4–77/8) and engineer of note, wrote several technical treatises. In one he quotes with approval the maxim of Gnaeus Domitius Corbulo, a commander renowned for his realistic training methods: 'Domitius Corbulo used to say that the pick (*dolabra*) was the weapon with which to beat the enemy' (*Strategemata* 4.7.2, cf. Tacitus *Annales* 13.35). This can only be a reference to the proven ability of the Roman army to build camps for itself. Obviously, recruits would have to be instructed in these military techniques, whereas fully trained soldiers would have to be exercised at fairly frequent intervals so as to maintain standards.

A scene from Trajan's Column (Scene CX) showing a marching-camp. A number of leather tents, designed for a tent-unit (*contubernium*) of eight men, are clearly visible within. (Reproduced from Lepper, F. and Frere, S. S., *Trajan's Column: A New Edition of the Chicorius Plates*, Sutton, Stroud, 1988)

Britain easily provides the largest number of practice-camps in the empire, the most common size being around 30.5 metres square. Often a mile or two away from the site of a fort and close to a Roman road, these sites are where troops trained in constructing marching-camps and in particular the most difficult sections of the camps, the corners and gateways.

The origins of Hadrian's Wall

Chronology

55 BC and 54 BC Gaius Iulius Caesar leads two punitive expeditions to southern Britain.

AD 43 Invasion and conquest of the southern part of Britain by the Emperor Claudius.

AD 119 Quintus Pompeius Falco, governor of Britannia, puts down a revolt in the province.

AD 122 Visit to Britannia by the Emperor Hadrian and soon afterwards work begins on the building of Hadrian's Wall.

AD 142/3 Building of the Antonine Wall from the Forth to the Clyde. Hadrian's Wall is abandoned until AD 163/4.

AD 208–11 The emperor Lucius Septimius Severus campaigns against the Maeatae and Caledonii, briefly reoccupying the Antonine Wall.

AD 367 The so-called 'Barbarian Conspiracy' – the Picts may at this time have overrun Hadrian's Wall.

c. AD 400 The *Notitia Dignitatum* catalogues the units commanded by the *dux Britanniarum* and includes a sub-section entitled 'also, along the line of the Wall' (*in partibus Occidentis* XL_{32-53}).

AD 407–11 Gradual withdrawal of the bulk of the remaining garrison of Britannia and, according to St Gildas (*De Excidio Britanniae* 18), a letter was sent by the emperor Honorius urging the people to see to their own defence.

c. AD 700 The *Ravenna Cosmographia* (107_{24-30}), which records the towns and rivers of the Roman world, lists the Wall forts from east to west.

AD 731 The Venerable Bede at Jarrow Monastery describes the Wall as 'eight feet in breadth, and twelve feet in height, in a straight line from east to west, as is clear to beholders to this day' (*Historia Ecclesiastica* 1.12).

According to Tacitus, Britain's reduction to a province was only achieved 'gradually' (*Agricola* 14.1). Indeed, some 80 years after the Claudian invasion, Roman Britain had no effective northern frontier that could be compared to the Rhine, Danube or Euphrates. Although the Stanegate, the Roman road connecting Corbridge with Carlisle, marked the northern limit of military occupation in Britain by the reign of Trajan, it was not a frontier system.

Since the reign of Claudius (AD 41–54), the security of the north had been founded on a treaty between Rome and the Brigantian queen, Cartimandua. In AD 69, however, her consort Venutius ousted Cartimandua and friendly relations between Rome and the Brigantes came to an abrupt end. In the cutting words of Tacitus, 'the kingdom was left to Venutius, the war to us' (*Historiae* 3.45). At a time of civil war in the empire, the governor, Marcus Vettius Bolanus (AD 69–71), was able to do little more than rescue the client-queen. There are hints of rather more military activity during his period of office than Tacitus reveals, but it seems highly improbable that Bolanus operated in Caledonia as the contemporary poet Statius implies (*Silvae* 142–9). The arrival of the new governor, Quintus Petillius Cerialis (AD 71–73/4), saw renewed activity in Brigantia. Tacitus (*Agricola* 17.1) fleetingly refers to Cerialis winning bloody battles against the tribe after campaigning widely in their territory. Although he built upon the successes of his energetic predecessors, credit for the eventual

The visible trace of the Stanegate that runs immediately south of the modern road leading to Chesterholm fort (*Vindolanda*), looking east – note the evidence of the pronounced camber and drainage ditches to either side. (Author's Collection)

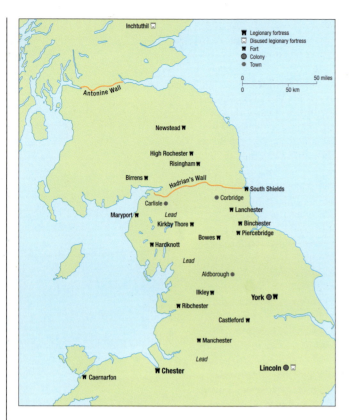

The principal military and civilian sites of northern Roman Britain, based on an original map by Guy de la Bédoyère. (© Copyright Osprey Publishing Limited)

subjugation of northern Britain is rightly given to Gnaeus Iulius Agricola, the father-in-law of Tacitus and governor of Britannia for seven years (AD 77/8–83/4). The new governor was neither a stranger to the province nor unaware of its problems, having served there as a military tribune during the Boudican revolt (AD 60–61) and later as legate of *legio XX Valeria Victrix*.

However, although the northern border may have appeared to be secure Hadrian's Wall did not stand in isolation. It was built in reaction to something or someone. Hadrian (r. AD 117–138) had a general policy of defining fixed limits for the empire, but a fresh outbreak of conflict in northern Britain at the outset of his reign might have been the immediate reason why the Wall was built. A tombstone from Ferentinum in Italy names Titus Pontius Sabinus, erstwhile *primus pilus* of *legio III Augusta*, who commanded *vexillationes* of *legiones VII Gemina, VIII Augusta* and *XXII Primigenia* on the 'expeditone Brittanica' (*ILS* 2726, cf. 2735) – see the glossary on pages 62–63 for a full explanation of terms. A reference in the text to his decoration by the deified Trajan makes it probable that this expedition to Britannia occurred in the latter part of Trajan's reign or under Hadrian.

For further evidence of a conflict in Britannia under Hadrian we can cite the tombstone inscription of Gaius Iulius Karus, prefect of the auxiliary unit *cohors II Asturum*, decorated *bello Brittanico* before his transfer to Egypt to serve as a tribune in *legio III Cyrenaica* (*AE* 1951.88). This revolt is also registered, albeit briefly, in a late fourth-century source as being one of the numerous troubles to afflict the new emperor, whereby 'the Britons could not be kept under Roman control' (*SHA Hadrian* 5.2). Further evidence is found in a letter written some 40 years after the event by Marcus Cornelius Fronto. Addressed to Marcus Aurelius (r. AD 161–180), his former pupil, Fronto consoles the emperor for the heavy losses his army had sustained in Parthia by recalling 'what a large number of soldiers were killed under your grandfather Hadrian by the Jews, what a number by the Britons' (22.2). A fragmentary tombstone from Chesterholm suggests that fighting took place precisely in the area where Hadrian was to have the Tyne–Solway system established:

T · ANN[IVS...] CENTVR[IO...] TVNGR[ORVM...] ... INBELL[O... INTER]FECTVS...

Titus Annius, a centurion of a legion serving as acting commander of the auxiliary unit *cohors I Tungrorum* at Chesterholm, may have been one of the casualties of this revolt (*inbell[o ... inter]fectvs*) that flared up at Hadrian's succession.

As for reasons for the uprising in Britannia, a Chesterholm–*Vindolanda* writing-tablet offers stark evidence for what could have caused local resentment. The derisive attitude to the *Brittunculi*, a previously unattested word that means something like 'nasty little Brits', and the derogatory comments on the fighting qualities of the 'naked Britons' (*nu[di] Brittones*) contained in the letter, suggests no great sympathy for the subject population (*Tab. Vindol.* II 164). From the turn of the second century, this memorandum presumably refers to Britons who had been recruited into the Roman army to form irregular units (*numeri*). The inscription of Titus Haterius Nepos, a prefect of cavalry, shows him holding a census of Britons in Annandale, just across the Solway Firth, not far from Chesterholm (*censito[ri] Brittonum Anavion[ens(ium)]*: *ILS* 1338). It may be that he was conscripting them into *numeri* for service on the frontier in Germania Superior, where ten *numeri* of *Brittones* were present at about the same time that the *Brittunculi* piece was written (*CIL* 13.8493, 16.19). The same Nepos was a correspondent of the Chesterholm prefect Flavius Genialis, the commander of *cohors I Tungrorum*, and asked him to come to Corbridge where he was probably stationed (*Inv.* 93/1379). According to Tacitus (*Agricola* 29.1, cf. 32.1) Britons had already been serving in the Roman army since the reign of Domitian. Indeed, Tacitus (*Agricola* 31.1) has Calgacus, the leader of the Caledonii at Mons Graupius, complaining of the forced levy (*dilectus*) whereby units were being raised in Britannia for service overseas.

The personification of Britannia appears for the first time on coins in the reign of Hadrian. One in particular, an *as* of AD 119 (*BMC* III Hadrian no. 1723), shows her in military garb, and in what appears to be a 'dejected' pose. This is often taken to imply the crushing of the rebels in Britannia by Quintus Pompeius Falco, Trajan's governor who had been left in the province.

Hadrian himself came to the province in AD 122 and, according to his biographer, 'he put many things to rights and was the first to build a wall, 80 miles long, to divide the Romans from the barbarians' (*SHA, Hadrian* 11.2). The line chosen for the Wall lay a little to the north of an existing line of forts along the Stanegate. This road had been constructed during the governorship of Agricola to link Corbridge on Dere Street, the arterial route up the eastern side of the province from the legionary fortress at York, with Carlisle on the western route north from the legionary fortress at Chester. Forts are known west of Carlisle and one east of Corbridge, but we cannot point to a frontier system across the Tyne–Solway isthmus prior to the construction of Hadrian's Wall.

Two fragments from an inscription, reused in a church in Jarrow just south of the Tyne, nicely encapsulate the whole business of the origins of the Wall and Hadrian's personal involvement:

> Son of all deified emperors, the Emperor Caesar Trajan Hadrian Augustus, after the necessity of keeping the empire within its limits had been laid on him by divine command … once the barbarians had been scattered and the province of Britannia recovered, added a frontier between either shore of Ocean for 80 miles. The army of the province built the wall under the direction of Aulus Platorius Nepos, Pro-Praetorian Legate of Augustus. (*RIB* 1051)

As a military tribune, Hadrian had seen service on the Danube and Rhine frontiers, and had first-hand experience of the Euphrates frontier as governor of Syria. Thus he was to some extent an expert on frontier defence. He also exhibited a keen interest in architecture. His reign opened with a crisis in Britannia and it was surely the Brigantes, with support from people across the Solway, who caused the trouble. This revolt was suppressed by Falco, but only after heavy Roman losses. Hadrian's subsequent visit to Britannia was part of a grand tour of the empire to supervise his policy of consolidating its frontiers as well as to reform training methods, ensure discipline and remove abuses in the army. Nevertheless, Roman attitudes to the Britons, the forced conscription and ensuing revolt, was at least part of the reason why Hadrian ordered the Tyne–Solway system to be built.

The anatomy of Hadrian's Wall

Hadrian's Wall consisted of four linear elements – the curtain-wall, the ditch, the Military Way, and the earthwork now known as the Vallum. Organic to this frontier system were the milecastles, turrets and forts that accommodated its garrison. Associated with this frontier system were the outpost forts to the north and the forts, fortlets and watchtowers that continued down the Cumbrian coast.

The Wall

The original length of Hadrian's Wall was to be 76 Roman miles (*c*. 70 miles) running along the northern edge of the Tyne Gap. From Newcastle upon Tyne, where a bridge was built and the site named *Pons Aelius* in honour of the emperor, to the crossing of the Irthing, the first 45 Roman miles (*c*. 41 miles) were to be built of stone to a width of 2.96 metres and perhaps 4.4 metres high to the walkway. The remaining 31 Roman miles (*c*. 29 miles) to the terminal point, just west of Bowness-on-Solway, was to be constructed of turf-blocks with a width at the base of 5.9 metres. Turf was a building material that was tried and tested, and its use in the western sector might indicate a need for speed of construction.

The Wall east of turret 48a (Willowford East) showing the horizontal offset where the Narrow Wall has been built on a Broad Wall foundation. (Author's Collection)

From a study of the Wall's structure there is evidence of a major revision in what is generally taken as the second full season of work – that is AD 124. This evidence consists of sections (e.g. turret 39a to turret 39b) where construction commenced for a stone curtain-wall of full width, but where the actual structure is only around 2.1 metres in thickness – known respectively as the Broad and Narrow Walls. Likewise, milecastles (e.g. 48 at Poltross Burn) and turrets (e.g. 48a at Willowford East) can be identified where preparations were made for a stone curtain-wall of greater breadth than was actually built. Before the project was completed the decision was taken to add forts to the line of the Wall and to speed up the construction process through the narrowing of the stone curtain-wall from 2.96 metres (10 Roman feet) to 2.35 or 1.83 metres (8 or 6 Roman feet). When this order was given all milecastles between the North Tyne and the Irthing had been erected as had most of the turrets, but work on the curtain-wall was not so well advanced.

Shortly after the decision to add the forts, and while they were still being built, another decision was taken, namely to add an earthwork behind the Wall. Further modifications to the original scheme were to follow. First, an extension was constructed down the Tyne from Newcastle to the fort at Wallsend in narrow gauge, but no Vallum, thereby increasing the length of the Wall to 80 Roman miles (*c*. 74 miles). Second, the new fort of Carrawburgh plugged the long gap between the forts of Chesters and Housesteads, as did that of Drumburgh between the forts of Burgh-by-Sands and Bowness-on-Solway. Third, there was a replacement of part of the

Turf Wall in narrow gauge stone curtain-wall, from milecastles 49 (Harrow's Scar) to 54 (Randylands). Finally, after the reoccupation of Hadrian's Wall under Marcus Aurelius, the remainder of the Turf Wall was rebuilt in stone and the Military Way constructed.

The Broad/Narrow Wall was erected on a foundation of rough slabs set in puddled clay. The stone used in its construction was mainly limestone. The stones were cut with roughly squared faces to allow them to be laid in regular straight courses, what stonemasons would recognise as 'coursed rubble'. These facing-stones had a tapered 'tail', which was embedded into the core; this was necessary to prevent the wall-face falling away from the core. At intervals it was deemed necessary to lay a flat course of slabs, which would tie the wall-faces more firmly into the core and level up for the next courses. Clay provided the main body of the core, with rubble serving as filler. Mortar was usually employed only to point the facing-stones, and then very sparingly. It seems one or two courses of facing-stones were laid, then the rubble and clay core added, then a couple more courses, more core, and so on. It is known that at least in some places the curtain-wall was rendered with plaster and given a lime-wash finish.

The Turf Wall was constructed of turf-blocks laid on a foundation of coursed turf three or four layers thick, although in certain sections this foundation consisted of rounded cobbles. Vegetius (3.8) specifies the optimum size of such turf-blocks, 1.5 by 1.0 by 0.5 Roman feet (444 × 296 × 148mm), but it is not known if the builders of the Turf Wall observed this rule. What little that survives of the Turf Wall suggests that its forward face had a steep incline, while its rearward face, at first vertical, continued upward at a steep incline. In height it was similar to the Broad/Narrow Wall, although a wattle parapet would have screened its walkway.

Although it is accepted that there was a protected walkway for patrolling along the Wall top, as the Rudge cup appears to suggest, we should not view the Wall as an elevated fighting platform due to its narrow width. Its height would have only provided a good, all-round visibility, including the ability to see to the bottom of the ditch to its front.

Ditch

Beyond the Wall there was a ditch, dug close to its north face except where it ran along the top of precipitous natural features, as it did from turret 33a (Sewingshields) to turret 45b (Walltown). The flat space between the two, the berm, was seldom less than 5.9 metres (20 Roman feet) wide for the Broad/Narrow Wall, whilst that in front of the Turf Wall was only 1.83 metres (6 Roman feet) wide. This served as a precaution both against the Wall slipping into the ditch and its being undermined by any excessive erosion of the ditch sides.

The ditch was, like most Roman military ditches, V-shaped in profile, the scarp and counter-scarp sloping up at an angle of 30 degrees to the vertical. In places along its length there are indications of a square-cut cleaning-channel (or 'ankle-breaker') at the bottom. The dimensions of the ditch vary from point to point, but the average is about 9–12 metres wide at the top and 2.66–2.96 metres deep. The material from the ditch was thrown to the north to form a broad mound or glacis, which considerably

The Rudge cup. Dated to c. AD 150, this small bowl appears to depict a stylised representation of the Wall as the band at the top names five forts in the western sector, Camboglans is Castlesteads. This is based on an original drawing by Guy de la Bédoyère.

The west wing-wall of turret 48a (Willowford East), looking east, showing the vertical off-set where the Broad wing-wall of the turret meets the Narrow Wall. (Author's Collection)

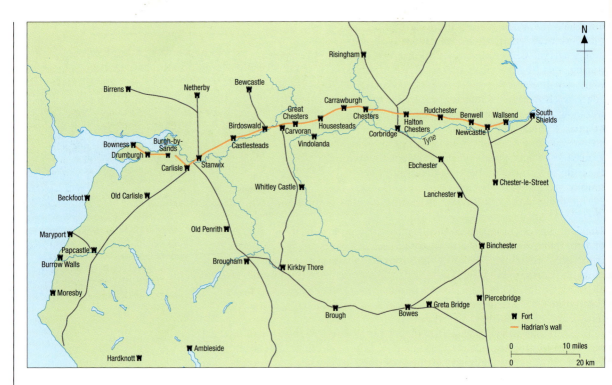

Hadrian's Wall and the forts along the northern frontier, based on an original map by Guy de la Bédoyère. (© Copyright Osprey Publishing Limited)

heightened the counter-scarp and tailed away gently northwards so as to afford no cover to an enemy. The subsequent building of those forts that sat astride the Wall led to the filling-in of stretches of the ditch (e.g. Birdoswald).

Military Way

Although clearly not part of the Hadrianic plan, for in places it overrides or runs along the top of the north mound of the Vallum, another linear element in the Tyne–Solway system was the Military Way, the road that ran roughly parallel to the Wall to the south. With the establishment of permanent garrisons on the Wall communication requirements had to be addressed. A number of spur roads linking the Military Way to forts, milecastles and turrets have been identified; its role was clearly to assist with communications along the frontier. Nevertheless, it does appear that this addition to Hadrian's Wall was not made until its reoccupation, perhaps resulting from experience gained on the Antonine Wall.

Surviving sections indicate that it was of standard construction, some 5.4–5.9 metres (18–20 Roman feet) wide with a pronounced camber and

The Wall and forward ditch, looking south-east towards turret 29a (Blackcarts), with the berm between the two. (Author's Collection)

drainage ditches on either side. As a rule, it was metalled with small stones, chiefly dark igneous rock such as basalt, and surfaced with fine gravel, resting upon a heavy bottoming of large cobbles with an under-layer of gravel bedding and edged with curbs of large stones. In areas with well-drained and firm subsoil little effort was made to provide boulder bottoming – only enough to ensure the correct cambered profile. On softer ground, the road builders either excavated down to the bedrock or 'floated' the road mound on a raft of sand or gravel.

With the Wall running along the top of the crags, the Vallum, looking east from milecastle 42 (Cawfields), occupies the low-lying ground to the south. The Vallum was not part of the original design. (Author's Collection)

Vallum

The Vallum was not part of the original plan but was added to the south of the Wall whilst construction work was still in progress. The decision to construct the Vallum was contemporary with, or post-dated, the decision to build the forts, though its actual construction may have preceded some or all of the forts. It diverges round Benwell, Haltonchesters, Birdoswald and Castlesteads, crosses the site of Carrawburgh, misses Carvoran altogether, and terminates at Newcastle not Wallsend.

This linear obstacle was designed as a broad flat-bottomed ditch, 5.4–5.9 metres wide at the top, 2.66–2.96 metres deep and 2.1 metres wide at the bottom with sides standing at 60 degrees. A berm of some 9–12 metres was cleared on each side of the ditch, bounded by mounds of earth, 2.66–2.96 metres in height, which were deliberately encased with stacked turf-blocks to retain the mounds' compactness. The surveyors on the spot modified this design to suit local conditions. Thus from north to south, the ditch and mounds of the Vallum presented a feature with an overall measurement of approximately 37 metres across. When the Vallum was completed, access to the Wall from the south was restricted to cobbled causeways opposite forts.

The purpose of the Vallum has been much debated, but it is conceivable that its primary function was to protect the rear of the frontier system from any internal hostilities. In some places the Vallum runs very close to the line of the Wall, while elsewhere it lies almost a mile away. Nevertheless, the ditch presented a formidable obstacle, while the mounds would have forced intruders into silhouette against the skyline, thereby making them more easily detectable before the Wall itself could be reached. The area between the Wall and the Vallum, therefore, provided a military zone to which access could be strictly controlled. However, towards the end of the second century this policy was relaxed as is evident from the settlements (vici) that began to spring up outside the forts.

Milecastles

These fortlets (c. 18m²) were built so that the Wall aligned with their north face. The milecastles provided a way through the Wall by means of their arched gateways with double-portal gates front and rear, the north gateway being topped by a tower. Built in stone – although those on the Turf Wall had originally had turf ramparts – they were routinely placed at intervals of one Roman mile (0.9 miles) regardless of the terrain.

Constructed to a standard plan, with one or two long buildings of timber or stone inside, they provided accommodation, if the space allocated per man in fort barrack-blocks is any indication, for eight to 32 men. The milecastles also contained a bread-oven, usually in the northwest corner, and in the opposite north-east corner a staircase to allow access to the rampart-walkway and the tower over the north gateway. Milecastles are numbered westward from Wallsend to Bowness-on-Solway.

The Vallum causeway just south of Benwell fort (*Condercum*), looking east. This crossing was installed with a substantial masonry gateway, the foundations of which are clearly visible. (Author's Collection)

The remains of the bread-oven situated in the north-west angle of the rampart of milecastle 48 (Poltross Burn). Bread-ovens were always positioned in the ramparts so as to reduce the risk of fire. (Author's Collection)

Turrets

Between each milecastle were two evenly spaced turrets (*c.* 6m^2), recessed into the Wall. These were watchtowers constructed at the same time as the foundations of the curtain-wall. They were built in stone, including those along the Turf Wall, and intended for temporary occupation by no more than eight men. Presumably higher than the curtain-wall, 9.5 metres high is not unreasonable, they served as observation posts and were also used for signalling back from the Wall.

A door in the south wall allowed access into the turret. In the centre of the ground floor was a hearth used for warmth and cooking. Access to the upper floor and walkway was by means of a ladder. Little evidence remains to show what the superstructure of the turrets would have looked like, but each turret or milecastle was in sight of its neighbour, thereby affording mutual protection whilst ensuring total surveillance along the frontier. As for milecastles, turrets are numbered westward from Wallsend to Bowness-on-Solway.

Forts

It was initially intended that the soldiers manning Hadrian's Wall would be based at the Stanegate forts, some as far as two miles to the south. While the Tyne–Solway system was under construction, however, the plan was changed and new forts built, where practicable, astride the Wall. We can see evidence of milecastles (45 at Greatchesters) and turrets (27a at Chesters, 36b at Housesteads, and 49a TW at Birdoswald) that have been started in their designated place, only to be overbuilt by forts.

With South Shields, Newcastle and Carvoran, there were a total of 17 forts on or close to the line of the Wall. On the line itself 12 had been planned and built initially, their spacing based on the distance that could be marched in half a day (*c.* 7 miles), but a further two were added (Carrawburgh and Drumburgh) and Carvoran rebuilt in stone towards the end of Hadrian's reign (*RIB* 1778, 1820). Carvoran was one of the Stanegate forts, which had been retained along with Carlisle, Chesterholm and Corbridge.

Fort defences of the period were devised for the use of hand-thrown weapons, namely throwing-spears or javelins (*pilum*). The effective range for javelins is estimated to have been 25–30 metres. At South Shields an untrained individual, throwing from the reconstructed west gateway and adjacent stretches of curtain-wall, has achieved distances of 15–20 metres. At least one V-shaped ditch, usually 5.4–5.9 metres wide at the top and 2.66–2.96 metres deep, surrounded a fort. The second line of defence was a moderately high stone curtain-wall, 1.2–1.5 metres in width and 3.6–4.4 metres in height to the rampart-walkway, with a narrower crenellated wall on top of that to protect the sentries. The circuit incorporated a series of towers at regular intervals and was backed with a bank of earth and rubble, or turf and clay. The bank added substantially to the circuit's strength and allowed access to the rampart-walkway at any point in an emergency. Inserted into these ramparts would be the bread-ovens (*clibani*), deliberately isolated from the internal buildings so as to reduce the risk of fire.

Milecastle 37 (Housesteads)

Built as part of Hadrian's Wall, milecastles were routinely spaced at intervals of one Roman mile regardless of geographical conditions. Most had gates in their north and south walls, making it technically possible to cross the Wall. This cutaway reconstruction is based on the well-preserved remains of milecastle 37 (Housesteads). On its east side stood a barrack-block of two rooms, the north serving as sleeping quarters and the south for the soldiers' equipment. With a total area twice the size of one of the barrack-block double-rooms in a fort, this would suggest the milecastle had a maximum garrison of 16 auxiliaries. These men came from the nearby fort at Housesteads. Note the Wall is shown here with patchy white rendering, which is testified by the archaeological record.

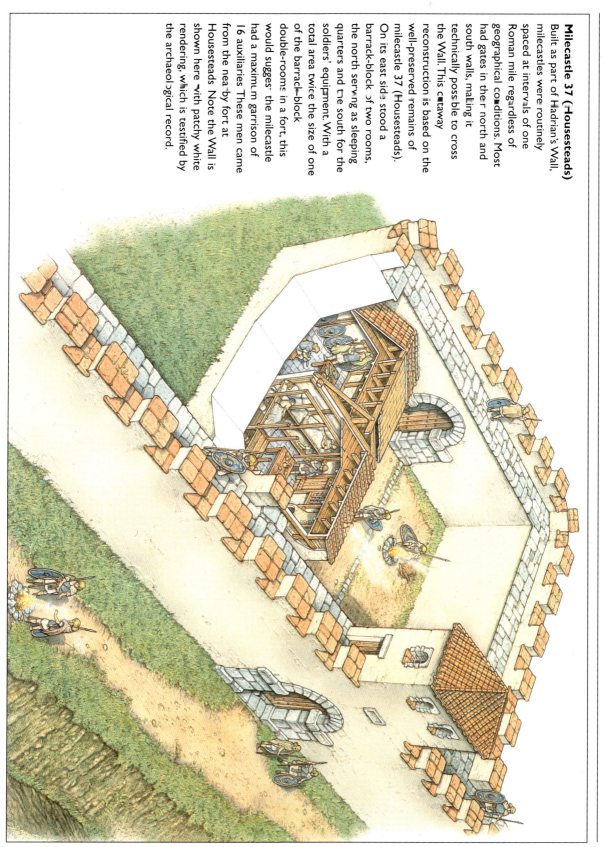

Turret 45a (Walltown) clearly recessed into the Wall, looking north-east. This turret is especially remarkable, for it was built as a free-standing look-out tower before the Wall was brought up to its east and west sides. (Author's Collection)

Immediately inside the rampart was the latrine block (*lavatrina*). Most excavated examples consist of a rectangular stone building situated at the lowest corner of the site where several drains converge and could be channelled to flush the latrine before discharging from the fort. The latrine block at Housesteads, which could perhaps seat some 16 men in comfort, reveals a good deal about the sanitary system of a fort. Although none of its seats survive, examples of stone or wood ones are known from other sites. As no fragments of the more durable stone seats exist, wooden ones are more likely. These would have taken the form of a continuous bench broken by key-hole-shaped slots. No provision was made for individual privacy and the total area of the Housesteads latrine may appear rather small for a garrison of at least 800 men.

Also in the *intervallum* would be a perimeter road. Access to a fort was through four fortified gateways with double-portal gates. Three of these, if the fort lay astride the Wall, gave access to the north, while those forts that utilised the Wall as their own northern rampart had only one gateway open to the north. Roads leading to a fort and those inside it were aligned with the gateways and the principle buildings. Internally, a fort was divided into three areas, the central range (*latera praetorii*), and the forward (*praetentura*) and rearward (*retentura*) ranges.

Forts, like fortresses, had a centrally placed headquarters building (*principia*), which faced the principle road (*via principalis*). This building, always in stone, served as the administrative and religious focus of the fort. It consisted of a paved courtyard surrounded on three sides by a portico of timber or stone columns, with ambulatories beyond. On the fourth side, that facing the entrance, stood an aisled cross-hall (*basilica*), where the dais (*tribunal*) from which the commanding officer presided over matters of routine and discipline stood. Behind this there was a range of five rooms. The central room housed the shrine (*sacellum*), which contained the imperial images, altars and standards of the garrison, below which was a small vaulted cellar in which was kept the ironbound chest that contained the soldiers' savings. Sentries were always posted outside to protect both the standards and the cash. The rooms on the tribunal side (left) were for the unit standard-bearers. Here they and their clerks kept the accounts and issued the troops' pay. The right-hand pair of rooms belonged to the *cornicularius* and his clerks. This was the home of army paperwork. The three central rooms, including the *sacellum*, had low stone screens with metal grilles fixed in them, so the objects of worship in the central shrine could be seen from outside, and the clerks could deal with the men without them crossing the threshold of their offices.

The interval tower between the south-east angle-tower and south gateway at Chesters fort (*Cilurnum*). The tower is built projecting inwards from the curtain-wall, a common feature of first- and second-century AD Roman fortifications. (Author's Collection)

On one side of the *principia* was the residence (*praetorium*) of the garrison commander. It normally took the form of a courtyard house with its own bath-suite and hypocaust heating, not unlike a small Mediterranean villa, where the commander, his family and household slaves would be accommodated with ease.

Also situated within the central range, but sited near one of the two side gateways, right (*porta principalis dextra*) and left (*porta principalis sinistra*), to provide convenient access, were the granaries (*horrea*), commonly paired, where the garrison's foodstuffs (*frumentatio*) were stored. According to Tacitus (*Agricola* 22.2) every fort in Britannia held

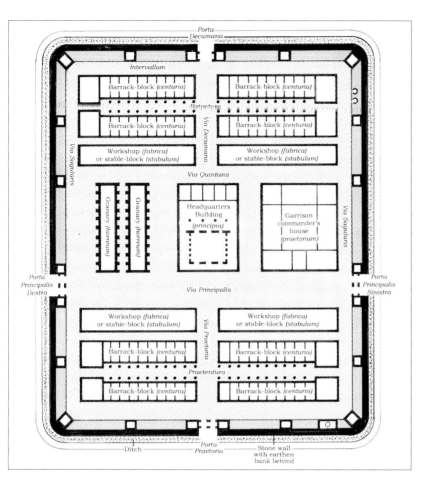

Inside the diagram (labels):

Porta Decumana

Intervallum

Barrack-block *(centuria)*   Barrack-block *(centuria)*

Retentura

Barrack-block *(centuria)*   Barrack-block *(centuria)*

Workshop *(fabrica)* or stable-block *(stabulum)*   Workshop *(fabrica)* or stable-block *(stabulum)*

Via Quintana

Via Sagularis

Via Decumana

Granary *(horreum)*   Granary *(horreum)*

Headquarters Building *(principia)*

Garrison commander's house *(praetorium)*

Via Sagularis

Porta Principalis Dextra

Via Principalis

Porta Principalis Sinistra

Workshop *(fabrica)* or stable-block *(stabulum)*   Workshop *(fabrica)* or stable-block *(stabulum)*

Via Praetoria

Barrack-block *(centuria)*   Barrack-block *(centuria)*

Praetentura

Barrack-block *(centuria)*   Barrack-block *(centuria)*

Ditch   Porta Praetoria   Stone wall with earthen bank behind

The principal features of a fort. The Latin terms are:

Principia – Headquarters building
Praetorium – Garrison commander's house
Horrea – Granaries
Centuriae – Barrack-blocks
Fabricae – Workshops
Stabuli – Stable-blocks

ample supplies to last one year, and examination of granaries has proved this to be correct. The visible characteristics of the stone-built granary were its raised floor, on longitudinal dwarf-walls or pillars; ventilation channels below the floor, which maintained the best conditions for storing grain; buttressed walls; and loading platforms.

A number of forts had hospitals (*valetudinaria*) in their central ranges. The normal arrangement was a number of small wards around a central corridor, with a reception area and operating theatre.

The forward and rearward ranges were taken up with barrack-blocks (*centuriae*), stable-blocks (*stabuli*) for draught and baggage animals, and workshops (*fabricae*) for the unit smith or armourer. Barrack-blocks, each holding a *centuria* or a *turma*, were usually half-timbered with low walls of sandstone rubble bonded with clay supporting timber uprights and frame. These were filled with wattle and daub. The roofs were of timber slatting (shingles), or thatch. Taking the form of a long and relatively narrow L-shaped building, approximately 10 metres wide and 40–50 metres long, each barrack was usually divided into ten two-roomed accommodation units (*contubernia*) with a larger apartment, forming the base of the L, for the centurion (*centurio*) of a *centuria* or the decurion (*decurio*) of a *turma*. A veranda ran the length of the building, often facing another building's veranda with a drain running between the two.

The officers' quarters were spacious and equipped with hearths, washing facilities and latrines, with timber-lined drainage channels leading to a pit filled with rubble, called a 'soak away', outside the building. Small pits were often dug beneath the floors, and they may have originally contained wooden chests in which personal documents or valuables were kept. It is not clear, however, how

A group of bread-ovens cut into the back of the earth rampart by the south gateway at Birdoswald fort (*Banna*). The surviving structures consist of a raised stone flagged floor and low stone walls upon which rubble and clay domes would have rested. (Author's Collection)

many people were actually housed within the officers' quarters. They may have been designed to accommodate not only the *centurio* or *decurio* and his slaves, but also their subordinate officers.

In a barrack-block designed to house an infantry *centuria* each *contubernium* accommodated eight men and their equipment. The outer room (*arma*) was for storing the soldiers' equipment and personal possessions, while the inner room (*papilio*) was where they slept, usually on palliasses. In a barrack designed to house a cavalry *turma* each *contubernium* accommodated three troopers, their equipment and their mounts. The outer room served as stables for the horses, the inner room accommodated the troopers. Hearths had been found in the inner rooms of some barrack-blocks, consisting either of a stone or tile setting with a semicircular stone or tile flue, while portable braziers may have been used in others. These were used for heating and cooking. The floors of these rooms were often of rammed earth or of pounded clay mixed with tile fragments. Small pits were often dug beneath the floor in both outer and inner rooms, and housed small wooden boxes, like the pits found in the officers' rooms, in which personal possessions were kept.

Bridges

In its course Hadrian's Wall had to negotiate three major rivers, the North Tyne at Chesters, the Irthing at Willowford, and the Eden near Carlisle, as well as several minor streams. The latter would have presented no particular problems, being dealt with the provision of large culverts in the Wall base of sufficient size to carry a full winter's spate. Archaeological evidence indicates that bridges carried the Wall across the Irthing and the North Tyne, but little is known about the bridge that spanned the Eden.

As a result of changes in courses of the rivers at Chesters and Willowford, sizeable remains of the abutments can still be made out at both these locations. In the early third century the bridge at Chesters, a small-scale affair carried on eight hexagonal stone-piers, was rebuilt. The replacement was a vastly more substantial stone bridge carried on three huge piers with pointed cutwaters. In like manner, the bridge at Willowford was also rebuilt.

The east gateway at Birdoswald fort (*Banna*), as seen from outside the fort, the best-preserved example on the Wall. Of particular interest are the double-portals and one of the springers (the part of an arch where the curve begins) for an arch over the northern passage. (Author's Collection)

Turret 18a (Wallhouses East)

Between each milecastle were two evenly spaced turrets. They were stone watchtowers built at the same time as the foundations of the Wall. This cutaway reconstruction shows turret 18a (Wallhouses East). A ladder was employed to reach the upper level of the turret and here the ladder-platform was found to be standing to full height, with six stone steps. As little evidence remains to show what the superstructure of turrets would have looked like, the form of the turret's roof is speculative. The general evidence from Trajan's Column is that many of the free-standing towers portrayed had pitched roofs. Facilities within the turret would have been very basic for its temporary garrison of eight auxiliaries. An open hearth was located next to the ladder-platform and, as indicated by the ample deposits of animal bones and coarse-ware pottery, was used by the soldiers for cooking their rations.

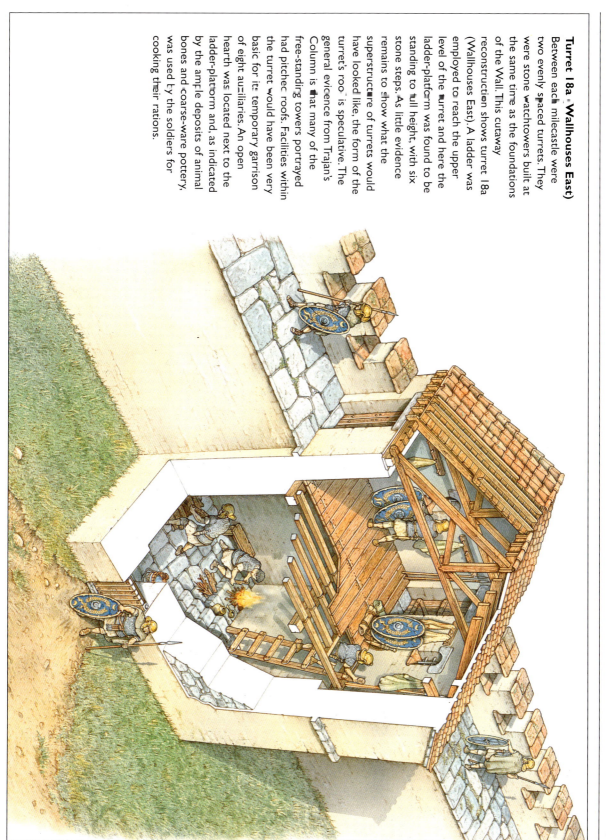

21

The cross-hall of the *principia* at Housesteads fort (*Vercovicium*). At the top centre of photograph is the *tribunal*, from where the commander of the garrison would have addressed his assembled troops. (Author's Collection)

Northern outposts

Some distances to the north of Hadrian's Wall were the outpost forts at Bewcastle, Netherby and Birrens, as well as those later established at Risingham and High Rochester close to the line of Dere Street. The first three, built in turf and timber, probably fall into the original scheme, for a road was built from milecastle 50 TW (High House) north to Bewcastle. On the return to Hadrian's Wall after the abandonment of the Antonine Wall, these first three outposts were reoccupied and were joined by the two to the east.

Although soldiers stationed here could monitor the local situation and feed back intelligence to the garrison on the Wall, their main role was to guard territory, presumably Brigantian, sundered from the rest of the province by the construction of Hadrian's Wall. Said by Tacitus (*Agricola* 17.1) to have been the most populous of all the tribes of Britannia, the Brigantes occupied much of what is now northern England, and their political centre of gravity lay in the Vale of York.

West coast defences

Although Hadrian's Wall terminated at Bowness-on-Solway, military control continued down the Cumbrian coast for at least a further 26 Roman miles (*c.* 24 miles) to Maryport by means of a series of fortlets and watchtowers, as well as five turf-and-timber forts (Beckfoot, Maryport, Burrow Walls, Moresby, Ravenglass). There was neither a curtain-wall nor a Vallum, the sea acted as the frontier and barrier.

Similar in design to those along the Wall, the fortlets and watchtowers were also spaced at intervals of one Roman mile and a third of a Roman mile respectively. The towers were built of stone from the outset and the fortlets of turf and timber. Unlike the Wall milecastles these milefortlets were never rebuilt in stone.

The frontier works continued beyond Maryport and may have run as far west as St Bees Head to control the movement of people across the Solway Firth. This coastal system, however, was not reoccupied after the withdrawal from the Antonine Wall. Its abandonment resulted from the realisation that Hadrian had been somewhat over-anxious with regard to the problems of security in the west.

The rear range in the *principia* at Wallsend fort (*Segedunum*), with part of the cross-hall to the right – note the sunken strong room beneath the *sacellum*, the central room of the rear range, which housed the unit standards and statues of the emperor together with altars to Iuppiter and Imperial Discipline. (Author's Collection)

Phases of construction

Hadrian's Wall bears all the hallmarks of a textbook plan, executed only in part before practical experience called for modifications. The evidence from extant structures and archaeological exploration suggest the following phases of construction:

1. Broad-gauge stone curtain-wall with stone milecastles and turrets from the Tyne to the Irthing
   Turf wall with turf-and-timber milecastles and stone turrets from the Irthing to the Solway coast
   Turf and timber milefortlets and stone towers, plus five turf and timber forts, along the Cumbrian coast
2. Decision to add forts to the line of the Wall
   The remaining stone curtain-wall and structures built in a narrower gauge
3. Vallum constructed
4. Forts at Carrawburgh and Drumburgh added
5. Wall extended down to the fort at Wallsend
   Decision to replace the Turf Wall from the Irthing to just west of milecastle 54 (Randylands) in stone
6. Bewcastle, Netherby and Birrens constructed
7. Move north to the Antonine Wall (AD 142)
8. Abandonment of the Antonine Wall (c. AD 164)
9. Rebuilding of the remaining Turf Wall in stone
   Military Way construction
   Risingham and High Rochester constructed

Here the important point is the clear evidence for alterations 'in the field'. Despite being a unique project, Hadrian's Wall demonstrates the flexibility and adaptability Roman military engineering.

Part of the north wing of the *praetorium* at Housesteads fort (*Vercovicium*), which includes a small dining room with a well-preserved hypocaust (underfloor heating) inserted in the fourth century. The officer in command, a *praefectus*, was a man of considerable social standing and his house reflects this position. (Author's Collection)

Reconstruction of the inner-room (*papilio*) of a barrack-block at Wallsend fort (*Segedunum*). Palliasses have been placed on low-lying beds. (Author's Collection)

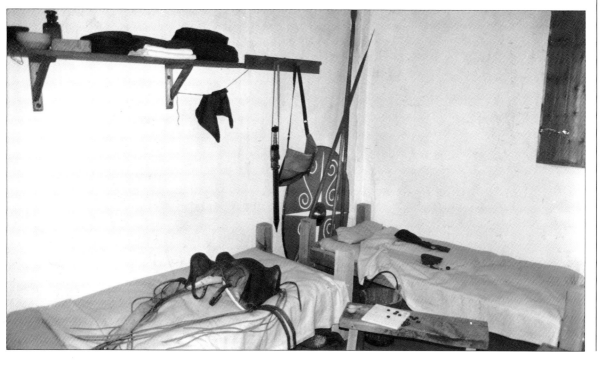

23

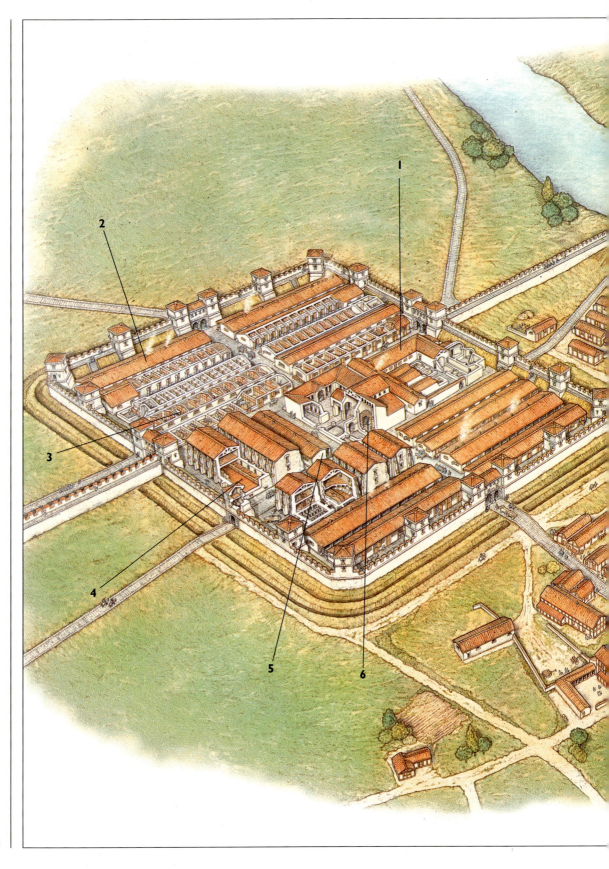

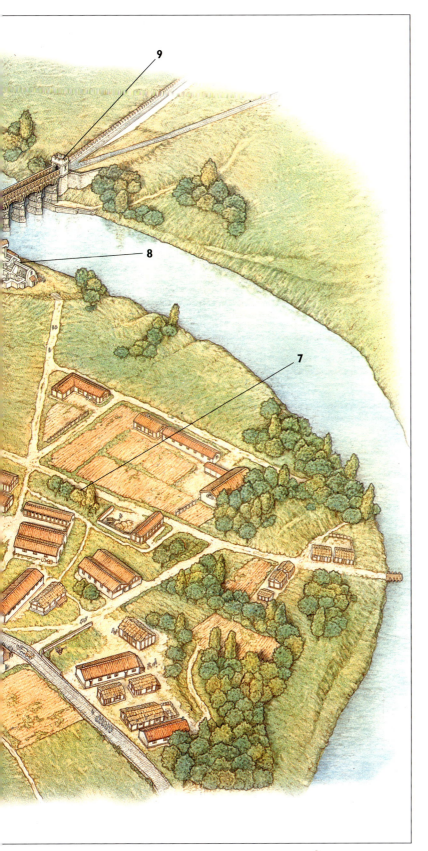

The cavalry fort at Chesters

A reconstruction panorama illustrating the cavalry fort at Chesters, the external bathhouse, and the original Roman bridge across the North Tyne. Also shown is the non-military settlement (*vicus*) on the southern slope between the fort and the river. As was common with non-military settlements, the *vicus* outside Chesters housed traders, both small-scale pedlars selling trinkets to the soldiers and merchants who held official contracts to supply the garrison with the thousand-and-one everyday commodities it required. Also present were basic service providers such as blacksmiths, cobblers, weavers, and makers and repairers of metal goods. Aligned with their short-axis facing onto one of the roads leading to the fort, the majority of buildings in the *vicus* conformed to the 'strip-building' type. Constructed of daub and timber, these were long narrow structures, with a commercial premises at the front, a yard, workshop or store behind, and then the living-quarters right at the back. They may have been an upper storey, providing extra accommodation or storage space. Frontages were generally open, but could be closed with shutters at night. Other buildings would have served as taverns, gambling dens and brothels.

1 Commandant's House
2 Stabling
3 Barracks
4 Granary
5 Workshops
6 *Principia*
7 *Vicus*
8 Bathhouse
9 Bridge abutment

The construction of Hadrian's Wall

Chronology

Some of the clues for working out the sequence and timing of the building of Hadrian's Wall have been mentioned. They are the filling-in of stretches of the ditch, dismantling of already built parts of the curtain-wall, milecastles and turrets in order to accommodate forts, the narrowing of the stone curtain-wall from broad gauge to narrow gauge, the extension to Wallsend, and the behaviour of the Vallum in diverging around forts. This gives a sequence of building, but no actual dates or timing.

The vital clue is supplied by the governor who was Hadrian's friend and chosen by him to build his Wall, Aulus Platorius Nepos. He came to Britannia not long before 17 July AD 122, as an auxiliary soldier discharged by the previous governor of Britannia, Quintus Pompeius Falco, received a *diploma* with that date and on it Nepos is named as governor (*CIL* 16.69). He came from a governorship of Germania Inferior, and it was from here that Hadrian came to Britannia in AD 122. Nepos was still in Britannia in AD 124 (*CIL* 16.70), but his governorship is unlikely to have extended later than the middle of AD 127. Lucius Trebius Germanus is named as governor of Britannia on a *diploma* issued on 20 August AD 127 (private collection, Munich), and this establishes the last possible date for the departure of Nepos.

For the initial phase the name of Nepos is found on building inscriptions from milecastles 37 at Housesteads (*RIB* 1634), 38 at Hotbank (*RIB* 1637, 1638) and 42 at Cawfields (*RIB* 1666) in the central sector, and on a wooden plaque found at milecastle 50 TW at High House (*RIB* 1935). For the modified scheme, his name appears on building inscriptions from the forts of Benwell (*RIB* 1340) and Haltonchesters (*RIB* 1427), as well as one from Chesterholm (*RIB* 1702). Unequivocally, Nepos is the only governor to be named on inscriptions from the Wall. Thus, Hadrian came to Britannia in AD 122 and, after personally surveying the situation, decided to build the Tyne–Solway system. Nepos is called over from Germania Inferior and commissioned by the emperor to take charge of the project. The three legions were summoned from their respective bases in Britannia and organised into work-parties. Nepos began Hadrian's Wall the same year, but while the project was under way he was compelled to alter the plans, building forts on the Wall and constructing the Vallum.

For each of these five years the effective working season would have been April to October as neither turf nor stone wall could have been constructed during the winter months. The turf was too weak then, and severe frosts ruled out mortar work. Frontinus (*De aquis urbis Romae* 2.123) recommends restricting the construction of aqueducts to the period April to October because of the effects of frost on setting mortar (the modern limit is *c.* 3° C). Besides, digging ditches and foundation-trenches would have been slow in frozen ground. As for assessing the likely work-rates for the project, we lack evidence regarding the labour-force and its capabilities. We do not know its precise size, or how it may have varied over the construction period, or the balance between skilled and less skilled, military or non-military. Other external factors to consider here include the effective working day, rest-periods and rest-days.

An inkling of the colossal amount of physical labour involved can be derived from experimental archaeology. At Baginton fort in the Midlands in 1966, a team of Royal Engineers reconstructed a turf-revetted rampart with a base 5.4 metres wide and a height of 3.6 metres to the walkway. It was calculated that to build the total length of the rampart with one-third earth fill, a circuit measuring some

283 metres, would require the cutting of 138,000 standard-size turf-blocks. With a labour force of 210 to 300 men, working ten hours per day under good weather conditions, the rampart could be completed, along with a double-ditch system, in nine to 12 days. Further experimental work done by the Royal School of Military Engineering suggests (assuming legionaries worked at 95 per cent of the efficiency of modern soldiers) that it would take 40 man-hours to build 100 metres of military road over grassland, 450 man-hours over heathland, and 600 man-hours over forest.

Materials

Work on a replica of Hadrian's Wall at Chesterholm, based upon the dimensions of the Broad Wall, has emphasised the amount of labour and material needed to build such a structure. This labour included the quarrying of facing-stones, stone cutting and dressing, the collection of stone rubble for the curtain-wall core, the procuring of vast quantities of lime mortar and the water for mixing it, obtaining timber for scaffolding, together with the transport of all these materials to the site. All told, the 14-metre-long replica needed some 400 tonnes of stone, as did the turret added to one end (based on the dimensions of turret 26b at Brunton). It also required 3,637 litres of water per day to mix the mortar.

Most of the building materials for the Tyne–Solway system were available locally, although some, for example the iron and lead needed for clamps, nails and fittings, were brought from elsewhere in Britannia.

The stone curtain-wall was faced with limestone, and needed around 3.7 million tonnes. In the central section this was easily obtained from local outcrops of limestone. Basalt, which forms the Whin Sill here, was not generally used as facing-stone because it was too hard for stonemasons to work easily into regular shapes. It was, however, sometimes used for large stones at the base of the Wall. In the west, when the Turf Wall was rebuilt in stone, local limestone was used for the first 7 Roman miles (c. 7 miles), and then the softer local red sandstone for the remainder. In the east some of the limestone would have been obtained locally, while the rest would have been ferried along the Tyne from quarries further afield. The facing-stone was probably roughly dressed at the quarry, to reduce the transportation of waste.

The rubble core of the stone curtain-wall consisted of any available stone set in puddled clay (75 per cent stone, 25 per cent clay), the latter material being secured from the ditch that was dug on the north side. Only for the milecastles was lime-based mortar used in the core. Despite being produced with a technique that was effective and quick, the use of a rubble core was liable to cause internal collapse, as Vitruvius (2.8.7–8) warns. This undoubtedly happened, for when sections of the curtain-wall were rebuilt they were set almost entirely in mortar.

Lime, the active ingredient of mortar, was produced from limestone, lumps of which were burnt with charcoal at very high temperatures in lime kilns. The process took some two to three weeks, the resultant lime being mixed with sand and water to produce mortar. Vitruvius (2.5.1) states that the proportion of sand to lime in a good mortar mix was 2:1 for river-sand and 3:1 for pit-sand. This mortar set very hard and was resistant to water and frost. The remains of lime kilns can be seen at numerous points on either side of the Military Way, and lime-burning is documented at Chesterholm (*Tab. Vindol.* II 156).

Water for slaking lime, mixing mortar and puddling clay would have come from one of the three major rivers in the Tyne–Solway isthmus and their associated tributaries. If moved in barrels, the provision of water for building alone would not only have been a labour-intensive operation, but it would have required a considerable amount of transport.

Timber – especially for lime-burning and scaffolding – would have been readily available since the area was then heavily forested, particularly on the lower-lying land and in the river valleys. When it came to construction the army always preferred to use long-lasting timber such as oak. If this was unavailable, alder, birch, elm and hazel were all used. For walls that were of wattle and daub, such as those of barrack-blocks, willow was an ideal timber for the wattles, although alder and birch were both good substitutes.

RIGHT **Early development of Hadrian's Wall**
A reconstructed scene showing the building of Hadrian's Wall at Limestone Corner, emphasising the various tasks performed by legionary work-parties. These were organised at century level under a centurion and allotted to a specific section of the Wall. Initially, some work-parties would involve themselves in clearing and laying-out, while other parties gathered building materials (timber and stone) from the immediate locality. Pack animals, wagons and carts, both legionary and local, would bring in materials (especially water) from further afield. Next, work would commence on digging the forward ditch (**A**) and laying the foundations of the curtain-wall (**C**) and those of its installations, in this example turret 29b (**B**). Further work-parties from the same century would follow behind, having been detailed to start work on the curtain-wall (**D**) and turret 29a (**E**). Note the absence of the Vallum, forts or Military Way. These features were not part of the original plan, which simply called for fortlets every Roman mile and two turrets between each one.

Estimated stone requirements in tonnes for the Broad Wall				
Feature	**Shaping-stone**	**Foundation-stone**	**Facing-stone**	**Core-stone**
Curtain	24,500	151,000	463,000	689,500
Structures	16,500	23,500	120,000	55,000
Estimated bonding material requirements in tonnes for the Broad Wall				
Feature	**Lime**	**Sand**	**Water**	**Core-clay**
Curtain	12,500	42,500	2,000	184,000
Structures	3,000	11,000	500	14,500

Notes: Length of the curtain wall: 24 Roman miles. Structures along it: 38 milecastles, 76 turrets, broad gauge, 1 bridge (Chesters)

ABOVE A scene from Trajan's Column (Scene LXII) showing water barrels being transported by a mule-cart. (Reproduced from Lepper, F. and Frere, S. S., *Trajan's Column: A New Edition of the Chicorius Plates*, Sutton, Stroud, 1988)

RIGHT A scene from Trajan's Column (Scene CXVII) in which a legionary work-party cuts and gathers timber. The cut timber is being stacked neatly ready for transportation. (Reproduced from Lepper, F. and Frere, S. S., *Trajan's Column: A New Edition of the Chicorius Plates*, Sutton, Stroud, 1988)

Builders

The construction work was undertaken by detachments of all three legions in Britannia, namely *vexillationes* from *legiones II Augusta* (from Caerleon), *VI Victrix pia fidelis* (from York) and *XX Valeria Victrix* (from Chester), together with help from the fleet (*classis Britannica*). The complement of each legion included a wide range of skilled men such as 'surveyors, ditch-diggers, architects, glaziers, roof-tile makers, plumbers, stonecutters, lime-burners, and woodcutters' (Paternus *Digest* 50.6.7). Vegetius (2.11) also lists legionary specialists. The most onerous tasks, however, appear to be not the actual construction work but its organisation and supervision.

Within the legion it was the responsibility of the *praefectus castrorum* to organise all construction work (Vegetius 2.10). As the legion's third in command – customarily an ex-*primus pilus* – this senior officer was the archetypal professional soldier. The building-work of the Wall, its installations (apart from the forts), and the works along the Cumbrian coast, were planned together and handled by the legionary work-parties. On both stone and turf sections the construction work was divided into lengths of 5–6 Roman miles (5–6 miles),

each the responsibility of a single legion. These legionary blocks were further subdivided and then allocated to individual centuries under the supervision of their respective centurions. Vegetius, in a passage describing what he calls a 'stationary camp' (*castra stativa*), says that during the construction of the ditch and rampart the 'centurions measure the work with ten-foot rods (*decempedae*), to check that no one through laziness has dug less than his share or gone off line' (3.8). Milecastles and turrets were generally built first, with work probably proceeding on the foundation of the curtain-wall and the digging of the ditch at the same time. Finally, it should not be forgotten that prior to actual construction-work the first tasks would have been setting-out, site clearance, site levelling, and assembly and preparation of building materials.

A centurial stone (*RIB* 1556) recording the construction of 24 paces (*P XXIIII*) of the rampart of Carrawburgh fort (*Brocolitia*) by a century under the command of Thrupo. (Author's Collection)

As each work-party completed its allotted section of work, a centurial stone was set into the Wall, or another structure, to record the fact. The extant building inscriptions for this initial phrase of the project provide a valuable record of the building of the turrets, milecastles and lengths of the curtain-wall. Take, for example, the following centurial stone:

LEG(IONIS) II AVG(VSTAE) COH(ORS) VII SV(B) CV(RA) …
From the Second Legion Augusta, the Seventh Cohort under the charge of …

This inscription (*RIB* 1932) is incomplete, but was found at milecastle 50 TW (High House). There is some indication of involvement on the part of the *auxilia* too:

C(OHORS) IIII LIN(GONVM) F(ECIT)
The Fourth Cohort of Lingonians built this

This inscription (*RIB* 2014) was found some 150 metres south of milecastle 59 (Oldwall), near the Vallum. It appears, therefore, that simpler operations probably employed auxiliaries for the actual excavation work. This unit, *cohors IIII Lingonum*, had originally been raised in Germania Superior (around Langres, eastern France) and was in Britannia by AD 103. Its only known place of garrison was Wallsend, where inscriptions (*RIB* 1299–1301) attest it for much of the third century, and where the *Notitia Dignitatum* (*in partibus Occidentis* XL$_{33}$) locates it at the turn of the fifth century.

Although there are visible structural differences in the curtain-wall, milecastles and turrets, there is no direct evidence, despite the building inscriptions, for allocating a particular variant to a legion. To date, the epigraphical evidence that has been found all belongs to that part of Hadrian's Wall where work was disrupted by the decision to build forts. The evidence for this disruption can still be seen at milecastle 37 (Housesteads). Here the north gateway had not reached the height of the impost caps (the element at the top of a pier that supports the arch) when the work was disrupted. Also, milecastle 42 (Cawfields) where the north wall was narrowed immediately beyond the side-walls of the milecastle, which, unusually, are not bonded in with the north wall. As the building inscriptions were erected over the gates, it is possible that in both cases one legion started building the milecastle and another completed the work. It is thus not possible to be certain that, for instance, *legio II Augusta* started building milecastles 37, 38 and 42 even though the building inscriptions from these structures bear its name (*RIB* 1634, 1637, 1638, 1666). In fact, it is much more likely that the milecastles were started by another legion only to be completed by *legio II Augusta*.

The major problem facing the Romans, according to the organisers of the Chesterholm replica project, was not the actual building of Hadrian's Wall but the logistics associated with its construction. It has been estimated that for every ten men actually involved in the construction work another 90 were needed to obtain and supply the raw materials. Local people may have been used for heavy labouring and carting. Indeed, if the work took five years to complete, it has been estimated that the delivery of materials would have needed a staggering 30,000 vehicles and drivers, 5,800 oxen and 14,200 mules or horses. On-site, however, the inherent flexibility of man-carrying makes it the most likely method of moving most materials, and this is certainly the construction method as depicted on Trajan's Column.

The builders of the Wall replica at Chesterholm also dug a ditch on its forward side. Digging through boulder clay, the team soon discovered that ditch digging was the toughest part of their project. In dry weather the boulder clay was found to be almost as hard as rock, in wet conditions like putty. Once the ditch was a few metres deep they had to cope not only with water from rainstorms but also with natural seepage through the sides, and if the water was not removed from the bottom of the trench it was impossible to work. By the same token, digging a ditch some 3 metres deep and 12 metres wide required triple shovelling. This technique had a man at the bottom that shovelled halfway up the bank, where a second man transferred the spoil onto the top lip and a third spread it out onto the glacis. Every so often the unfortunate diggers came across glacial boulders, weighing anything up to a tonne, and these had to be split before removal. This was a relatively easy task if the boulders where sandstone, a difficult one if they were basalt.

The north gateway of milecastle 37 (Housesteads) as seen from inside the milecastle. The arch stones have been partially restored. (Author's Collection)

A scene from Trajan's Column (Scene LX) in which legionaries, working in body armour but bare-headed, dig ditches and cut and handle turf-blocks – note the rope sling to carry turf-blocks on their backs and the use of baskets to move soil. (Reproduced from Lepper, F. and Frere, S. S., *Trajan's Column: A New Edition of the Chicorius Plates*, Sutton, Stroud, 1988)

ABOVE The ditch and glacis at Limestone Corner looking north-east, both of which are littered with abandoned boulders and blocks. The rock here simply proved too hard and the builders gave up their bid to complete the forward ditch. (Author's Collection)

LEFT An abandoned basalt boulder squats defiantly in the ditch at Limestone Corner, complete with cuttings for splitting-wedges. This rock was broken up by chiselling holes into it and inserting iron or wooden wedges, the former hammered, the latter expanded by having water poured upon them. (Author's Collection)

FOLLOWING PAGE **Anatomy of the Wall**
A reconstructed aerial view of Hadrian's Wall at Birdoswald, showing the fort as it may have appeared after the Turf Wall was rebuilt in stone after AD 163/4. The earthworks of the Vallum are visible in the foreground, and on the eastern end of the spur sits milecastle 49 (Harrow's Scar). South of the fort, at the foot of a bold scarp, snakes the river Irthing with the Roman bridge at Willowford immediately due east of the milecastle. Pollen evidence shows that when the builders of the Wall arrived here they found dense woodland with a fairly deep morass in the middle. Birch and alder grew on the wetland, with oak on the drier slopes towards the Irthing. Hazel thrived in both areas and would have been a suitable material, as were birch and alder, for the wattlework parapet that probably adorned the top of the original Turf Wall. Note it is impossible to be certain how the stone Wall was finished at the top, but a rampart walkway with a crenellated breastwork on its northern edge may be considered the most likely.

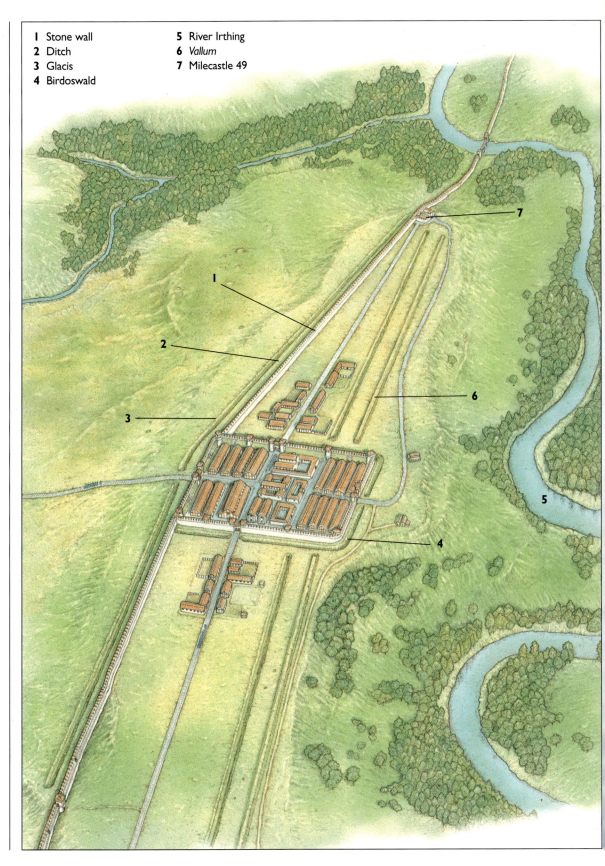

1 Stone wall
2 Ditch
3 Glacis
4 Birdoswald
5 River Irthing
6 *Vallum*
7 Milecastle 49

The function of Hadrian's Wall

Roman Britain should not be looked at in isolation from the rest of the empire, and the Tyne–Solway system symbolises the imperatives of Hadrian's overall frontier policy. His predecessor, Trajan, wished to secure conditions of peace and stability in the empire and saw territorial acquisition, and the consequent ability to police old enemies, as the means to this end. Ultimately, Trajan was faced with a 'worst-case scenario'. That is, the troops required to achieve this goal were sufficient if war was not conducted simultaneously on more than one front. By the end of his reign, however, Trajan was faced with completing and securing his new eastern conquests, stabilising his recent success in Dacia and 'holding the line' elsewhere. In AD 117, these needs could not all be handled with a finite supply of troops. Hadrian, too, wanted stability on the frontiers, but he was no warrior-emperor like Trajan. Hadrian's policy, as his biographer in the *SHA* clearly states, was to separate the Romans from the barbarians by means of visible boundaries. Trajan's death brought imperial expansion to an end and the results of Hadrian's visit to Britannia show that the new emperor's view of imperial security, whilst no less dynamic than that of his predecessor, was very different in its expression.

Hadrian's Wall was conceived as an enhancement of, rather than a replacement for, the Stanegate, where in the first construction plan, the main bodies of troops for garrison duties and police work were retained in the existing forts. The milecastles were, in reality, fortified gateways and the nature of the first plan suggests the principal purposes were observation and the supervision of crossing in either direction. Such duties were to be carried out

Milecastle 42 (Cawfields) looking north-east, which was clearly built in the lower ground, named Hole Gap, situated between two stretches of crag – note the solid remains of the south gateway. (Author's Collection)

The conspicuous remains of the internal stairway at milecastle 48 (Poltross Burn), which gave access to the rampart-walkway and the tower above the north gateway. This stairway is exceptional and has not been found in other milecastles. (Author's Collection)

by small groups of soldiers housed in the milecastles and turrets. Yet there is a major problem in any interpretation of the function of the milecastles, namely the absence of causeways in front of their north gateways. Certainly the lack of causeways across the ditch, unless timber bridges were employed, clashes strongly with the provision of so many gateways through the Wall. The latter suggests that this was to be an open frontier, the former a closed barrier.

This role of surveillance and, perhaps, supervising movement, could obviously be more effectively discharged if the frontier had a strong visual command of the territory in which it was set. The Stanegate lacked this advantage because of its close relationship with the valleys of the Tyne, Irthing and Eden rivers. The line selected for Hadrian's Wall, therefore, advanced northwards to occupy the northern crests of those valleys, and thus acquire a command of territory. The Wall would thus utilise the Whin Sill, a basaltic outcrop forming a line of north-facing crags, in its central sector. Similarly, in the eastern sector it would run along the north rim of Tynedale, while in the western sector it would follow the north side of the valley of the Irthing. Thus the initial plan was to build a linear barrier from Newcastle to Bowness-on-Solway, which was equipped with a fortlet every Roman mile and a pair of watchtowers between each pair of fortlets.

However, Hadrian's Wall turned out rather differently from the original plan. In the first Hadrianic scheme the two functions of frontier defence and frontier control had been separated, with the role of defence resting upon the garrisons in the Stanegate forts and the role of control being undertaken by the soldiers in the milecastles and turrets. In the second Hadrianic scheme, both functions were focused on the Wall itself. This is how the Tyne–Solway system developed whilst under construction.

It must be stressed that the Wall was a barrier and not a fighting-platform. The walkway, allowing for a parapet some 60 centimetres (2 Roman feet) in width, was only some 1.83–2.35 metres (6–8 Roman feet) wide on the Broad Wall alone. There was scarcely room to pass behind a man and the only access points to bring up reinforcements were the milecastles and turrets, some 500 metres apart, via their narrow stairways. Moreover, there was no provision on the Wall for enfilading fire from projecting towers, nor positions from which to mount artillery. The Roman army only fought from behind the shelter of walls as a last resort, its guiding philosophy being one of dealing with an enemy in the open. The addition of the forts to the line of the Wall allowed for the maintenance of tighter supervision and closer observation, and gave the garrison the ability to patrol more effectively to the north.

Renewed warfare in the mid-120s AD may have led to the decision to emplace forts in the wall, and fundamental to any consideration of how Hadrian's Wall functioned is the perception of threat to Rome's control of the frontier. As we have seen, the northern tribes were not necessarily as peaceful as has usually been presumed. The latter part of the second and the early years of the third century AD saw a series of disturbances in Britannia. In AD 161, at the beginning of the reign of Marcus Aurelius, 'war was threatening in Britannia … and Calpurnius Agricola was sent to deal with the Britons' (*SHA, Marcus Aurelius* 8.7–8). Again, in AD 169/70, 'the Britons were on the verge of war' (*SHA, Marcus Aurelius* 22.1). It was some three years later, towards the end of Sextus Calpurnius Agricola's governorship, that the Antonine Wall was abandoned and Hadrian's Wall was fully reoccupied (*RIB* 1137, 1149, cf. 1389). Cassius Dio, writing a few decades later, called it 'the cross wall that splits the island in two' (77.12.1). The reign of Commodus opened with a major incursion when 'the tribes in the island crossed the wall (*to teîchos*) that separated them from the Roman legions, did a great deal of damage, and cut down a general (*strategos*) and his troops' (Dio 73.8.2). Although Dio does not specify which wall was crossed, the destruction deposits found at Haltonchesters dating from around AD 180, its neighbour Rudchester, and also at Corbridge two miles to the south, suggest it was Hadrian's Wall. If this was the case, then the invaders moved south down Dere Street, sacking the sites in their path. How far south they reached is unknown, but the Roman commander killed was of senior rank and may have been the legate from York. Of interest here is the late second-century inscription (*RIB* 755.A) that records

A scene from Trajan's Column (Scene XXXII) in which auxiliaries, positioned on a rampart walkway, hurl javelins at Dacian warriors who are assaulting their fort. Of particular interest are the various devices on the shields of the auxiliaries. (Reproduced from Lepper, F. and Frere, S. S., *Trajan's Column: A New Edition of the Chicorius Plates*, Sutton, Stroud, 1988)

A nocturnal attack on the wall

An attack on the Wall based on the major incursion by the Caledonii at the beginning of Commodus' reign (c. AD 181), which resulted in the destruction (by fire) of Haltonchesters, Rudchester and Corbridge. This conjectural reconstruction shows the north gateway of the fort at Rudchester under assault while a diversionary attack is delivered against turret 13b to the fort's immediate west. Although Rudchester was built for a *cohors quingenaria equitata* (name unknown), the garrison would have been below its official complement due to other commitments such as manning the nearby milecastles and turrets or support duties further afield. Moreover, it is important to note that Roman military installations of the first and second centuries were not primarily intended as defensive sites, did not possess especially strong fortifications, and were not built on formidable positions. Normally, the army expected to defeat its enemies in the open field, and even heavily outnumbered garrisons exhibited a willingness to come out and fight more numerous attackers.

the burial at Ambleside of two men, a retired centurion and an accounts clerk (*actarius*), probably father and son, the latter having been killed in the fort by the enemy.

ABOVE The reconstructed west gateway at South Shields (*Arbeia*), as seen from inside the fort, with the two stairways leading up to the rampart walkway. (Author's Collection)

Other late second-century inscriptions demonstrate that punitive campaigns were conducted north of Hadrian's Wall. An altar found at Kirksteads, near Stanwix fort, was erected by a legate of *legio VI Victrix* to give thanks for 'the successful outcome of action conducted beyond the Wall' (*RIB* 2034). A prefect of cavalry dedicated an altar at Corbridge after his unit 'slaughtered a band of Corionototae' (*RIB* 1142), a people otherwise unrecorded but probably a branch of the Brigantes. Nevertheless, in AD 197 the governor of Britannia, Virius Lupus, did not have enough strength, presumably as a result of the civil war between Septimius Severus and his rivals, to mount an offensive against the Maeatae and Caledonii and thus 'brought peace for a considerable sum of money' (Dio 75.5.4). Ten years later, his successor was 'winning the wars in Britannia' (Dio 77.10.6). Yet despite Septimius Severus' subsequent campaigns against the northern tribes, we still hear of the Maeatae and Caledonii rising in 'rebellion' (Dio 77.15.1–2). And so the fortunes of Rome on her northern frontier were inextricably linked with imperial events elsewhere and the attitude of the northern tribes either side of the Wall.

The garrison of Hadrian's Wall

It was the *auxilia*, and not the legions, who actually garrisoned the frontier. By the time the Tyne–Solway system was completed, as much as a third of all the *auxilia* in Britannia were stationed in the Wall zone (i.e. *c.* 9,000 men). The fundamental distinction between legionary and auxiliary, especially during the early empire, is an important one. The legionary was a Roman citizen. The auxiliary, on the other hand, was a non-citizen (*peregrinus*), Roman citizenship and *conubium* (that is, regularisation of existing or future marriages, so that any children would be citizens also) was a privilege granted to him after 25 years service. The promise of citizenship was a powerful inducement to join, and its grant was recorded in the auxiliary's *diploma*, the small bronze folding-tablet that was conferred on him upon his honourable discharge from the army. The volunteer had to prove he was freeborn, and had to pass a medical. The optimum age was between 18 and 23 – in Britannia the oldest known auxiliary recruit is a soldier of *cohors IIII Gallorum* at 30 (*RIB* 1249). Despite their lack of citizenship, however, we should not view the members of the *auxilia* as second-rate troops. As well as being used as the primary frontier garrisons, they were also placed first in the front line on the battlefields.

Tacitus (*Annales* 4.47) once remarked of a *cohors Sugambrorum* under Claudius, that it was still 'Germanic' although fighting far from home in Thrace. Additional information comes from Tacitus' account of the civil war. In AD 69, when Vitellius entered Rome, his army also included 34 auxiliary cohorts 'grouped according to nationality and type of equipment' (*Historiae*

A turf-and-timber fort, as depicted on Trajan's Column (Scene XX), showing detail of the installation's rampart walkway, which was constructed out of timber, and crenellated wall. (Reproduced from Lepper, F. and Frere, S. S., *Trajan's Column: A New Edition of the Chicorius Plates*, Sutton, Stroud, 1988)

2.89). Auxiliary units were recruited from warlike peoples within or on the periphery of Roman control, notably Gallia Belgica and Lugdunensis, Germania Inferior, and Pannonia. The members of *cohors II Tungrorum*, for instance, had been originally raised from among the Tungri tribe who inhabited the north-western fringes of the *Arduenna Silva* in Gallia Belgica (Ardennes Forest, Germano-Belgic border). Under the Julio-Claudian emperors it was quite common for such units to be stationed in or near the province where they were first raised. However, the events of AD 69–70, with the mutiny of a large proportion of the auxiliaries serving on the Rhine, led to a change in this policy. Although the Romans did not abandon local recruiting, they did stop the practice of keeping units with a very strong ethnic identity close to their homelands. Naturally, by the late first century, units were being kept up to strength by supplements from the province where they were now serving or areas adjacent to it. Such units retained their ethnic identities and names, even if they enlisted new troops from where they were stationed. The epitaph of Sextus Valerius Genialis tells us that he was a trooper in *ala I Thracum*, and his three-part name reveals that he was a Roman citizen. But it adds that he was a 'Frisian tribesman' (*RIB* 109). So, Genialis came from the Lower Rhine, served in a Thracian cavalry unit stationed in Britannia and styled himself Roman.

Auxiliary units were of three types: *alae* consisting solely of cavalry, *cohortes peditatae* consisting solely of infantry, and mixed units of both foot and horse called *cohortes equitatae*. All these units were based on the *centuria*, the infantry century commanded by a *centurio*, and the 32-strong *turma*, the cavalry troop commanded by a *decurio*. The *cohors peditata* was either 500-strong (*quingenaria*) or 1,000-strong (*milliaria*). The former was clearly based on the legionary cohorts II–X as it consisted of six *centuriae* each 80 men strong, but unlike a legionary cohort a prefect (*praefectus cohortis*) commanded it. The latter, unlike the 'double centuries' of the first cohort (*prima cohors*) of a legion, was of ten *centuriae* each eighty men strong, a total of 800 men under the command of a tribune (*tribunus*). Likewise, the *cohors equitata* was either *quingenaria* or *milliaria*. The former consisted of six *centuriae* and four *turmae*, a total of 480 men and 128 troopers under a *praefectus cohortis*. The latter consisted of ten *centuriae* and eight *turmae*, a total of 800 men and 256 troopers under a *tribunus*. The *ala* would be either of 512 troopers in 16 *turmae* (*quingenaria*), or of 768 troopers in 24 *turmae* (*milliaria*). A prefect of cavalry (*praefectus alae*), however, commanded both.

As with the legions, auxiliary units had numbers and names, and could also accumulate an impressive set of titles for bravery and loyalty. Those units raised in the western provinces generally took their names from a tribe or region, those in the east from a city. There were, for example, five cohorts raised in Gaul, *cohors I–V Gallorum*, possibly just before the invasion of Britain in AD 43. Again, like the names of legions their names become embroidered with the unit's history. For example, *ala Gallorum et Thracum Classiana invicta bis torquata civium Romanorum* was raised in Gaul during the reign of Tiberius (AD 14–37). It took the title *Classiana* from the name of its first commander, the Gallic nobleman Iulius Classianus. The addition of a contingent of Thracians gave it *et Thracum*. It gained the title *invicta*, invincible, and the honour of a torque twice, hence *bis torquata*, and a block grant of citizenship as a reward for meritorious conduct on the field of battle to all of its serving men, hence *civium Romanorum*. Henceforth the unit itself employed the designation *c(ivium) R(omanorum)*, but all future recruits remained non-citizens until their honourable discharge as the citizenship went only to those serving at the moment of the reward. The first torque was gained possibly during the Flavian period and the second during the reign of Trajan or that of Hadrian, on both occasions in Britannia. As military decorations were not available for the non-citizen, the torques were awarded to the unit as a whole and hence carried on its standards.

The probable garrisons of forts on the Tyne-Solway system			
Fort	**Size** *Acres (hectares)*	**Garrison** *Second century AD*	**Garrison** *Third century AD*
Wall			
South Shields I (*Arbeia*)	3.75 (1.52)	*ala I Hispanorum Asturum quingenaria* (RIB 1064)	
South Shields II (*Arbeia*)	5.16 (2.09)		Ca: *cohors V Gallorum quingenaria eq* (RIB 1070.B) SA: *cohors V Gallorum quingenaria eq* (RIB 1060)
Wallsend (*Segedunum*)	4.10 (1.66)	MA: *cohors II Nerviorum quingenaria cR* (RIB 1303)	*cohors IIII Lingonum quingenaria eq* (RIB 1299-1302, 2411.109, 2476.1-2)
Newcastle (*Pons Aelius*)	5.64 (2.28)	AP: *vexillationes of legiones VI Victrix pf* *& XX Valeria Victrix* (RIB 1322)	Ca: *cohors I Ulpia Traiana Cugernorum* *quingenaria cR* (RIB 1322.C)
Benwell (*Condercum*)	5.64 (2.28)	AP: *vexillatio of legio II Augusta* (RIB 1330) MA: *cohors I Vangionum milliaria eq* (RIB 1328)	SS: *ala I Hispanorum Asturum quingenaria* (RIB 1337) SA: *vexillatio of classis Britannica* (RIB 1340) Go: *ala I Hispanorum Asturum quingenaria* (RIB 1334)
Rudchester (*Vindobala*)	4.50 (1.82)		*cohors I Frisiavonum quingenaria* (RIB 1395)
Haltonchesters (*Onnum*)	4.30 (1.74)		*ala I Pannoniorum Sabiniana quingenaria* (RIB 1433)
Chesters (*Cilurnum*)	5.75 (2.33)	H: *ala Augusta quingenaria ob virtutem* *appellata* (RIB 1497.C) AP: *vexillatio of legio VI Victrix pf* (RIB 1460-1) MA: *cohors I Vangionum milliaria eq* (RIB 1482) MA: *cohors I Delmatarum quingenaria* (RIB 1496.A) Co: *ala II Asturum quingenaria* (RIB 1463-4)	SS: *ala II Asturum quingenaria* (RIB 1462) E: *ala II Asturum quingenaria* (RIB 1465-6)
Carrawburgh (*Brocolitia*)	3.50 (1.42)	H: *cohors I Aquitanorum quingenaria* (RIB 1550) MA: *vexillatio of cohors II Nerviorum* *quingenaria cR* (RIB 1538) Co: *cohors I Ulpia Traiana Cugernorum* *quingenaria cR* (RIB 1524)	Ca: *cohors I Batavorum quingenaria eq* (RIB 1544-5) MT: *cohors I Batavorum quingenaria eq* (RIB 1553)
Housesteads (*Vercovicium*)	5.00 (2.03)	H: *cohors I Tungrorum milliaria* (RIB 1632.A)	SS: *cohors I Tungrorum milliaria* (RIB 1632.B) SA: *cohors I Tungrorum milliaria with cuneus* *Frisiorum Vercoviciensium Severiani* *Alexandriani & numerus Hnaudifridi* (RIB 1576, 1578-80, 1584-6, 1591, 1594, 1598, 1618-19)
Greatchesters (*Aesica*)	3.36 (1.36)	H: *cohors VI Nerviorum quingenaria* (RIB 1731) MA: *cohors VI Raetorum quingenaria* (RIB 1737)	SA: *cohors II Asturum quingenaria eq* *with vexillatio gaesatorum Raetorum* (RIB 1724, 1738)
Carvoran II (*Magnis*)	3.70 (1.50)	MA: *cohors I Hamiorum sagittariorum* *quingenaria* (RIB 1792)	*cohors II Delmatarum quingenaria* (RIB 1795)
Birdoswald (*Banna*)	5.33 (2.16)		SS: *cohors I Thracum quingenaria equitata cR* and *cohors I Aelia Dacorum milliaria* (RIB 1909) Ca: *cohors I Aelia Dacorum milliaria* (RIB 1892) E: *cohors I Aelia Dacorum milliaria* (RIB 1914) MT: *cohors I Aelia Dacorum milliaria* (RIB 1875, 1896, 1929.A) Go: *cohors I Aelia Dacorum milliaria* (RIB 1893) Ga: *cohors I Aelia Dacorum milliaria* (RIB 1882-3, 1886) A: *cohors I Aelia Dacorum milliaria* (RIB 1885) P: *cohors I Aelia Dacorum milliaria with* *numerus venatores Bannienses* (RIB 1905, 1929.B)

Castlesteads (*Camboglanna*)	3.75 (1.52)	H: *cohors IIII Gallorum quingenaria eq* (RIB 1979-80)	Go: *cohors II Tungrorum milliaria eq cl* (RIB 1981-3, 1999)
Stanwix (*Petrianis*)	9.32 (3.78)	*ala Augusta Gallorum Petriana milliaria cR bis torquata*	*Ala Augusta Gallorum Petriana milliaria cR bis torquata* (RIB 2411.84)
Burgh-by-Sands (*Aballava*)	4.90 (1.98)		Go: *cohors I Nervana Germanorum milliaria eq* with *cuneus Frisionum Aballavensium Philippianorum* (RIB 882-3, 2041) Ga: *cohors I Nervana Germanorum milliaria equitata* with *numerus Maurorum Aurelianorum Valeriani Gallienique* (RIB 2042)
Drumburgh (*Concavata*)	2.00 (0.81)		*cohors II Lingonum quingenaria eq*
Bowness-on-Solway (*Maia*)	7.00 (2.84)		

Coastal

Beckfoot (*Bibra*)	3.25 (1.32)	MA: *cohors II Pannoniorum quingenaria* (RIB 880)	
Maryport (*Alauna*)	6.50 (2.63)	H: *cohors I Aelia Hispanorum milliaria eq* (ILS 2735 with RIB 823) AP: *cohors I Delmatarum quingenaria* (RIB 832, 850) MA: *cohors I Baetasiorum quingenaria cR ob virtutem et fidem* (RIB 830, 837-8, 842-3)	*cohors III Nerviorum quingenaria* (RIB 879.A) Go: *vexillatio of legio XX Valeria Victrix* (RIB 854)
Moresby (*Gabrosentum*)	3.70 (1.50)	H: *cohors II Lingonum quingenaria eq* (RIB 798, 800) MA: *cohors II Thracum quingenaria eq* (RIB 797)	*cohors II Thracum quingenaria eq* (RIB 804)
Ravenglass (*Tunnocelum*)	3.70 (1.50)	*cohors I Aelia classica quingenaria*	*cohors I Aelia classica quingenaria*

Stanegate

Corbridge I		H: *ala Augusta Gallorum Petriana milliaria cR bis torquata* (RIB 1172)	
Corbridge II (*Coria*)		AP: *vexillatio of legio II Augusta* (RIB 1147-8) MA: *vexillationes of legiones VI Victrix pf & XX Valeria Victrix* (RIB 1137, 1149)	SS: *vexillatio of legio VI Victrix pf* (RIB 1163)
Chesterholm III (*Vindolanda*)	4.00 (1.62)	H: *cohors I Tungrorum milliaria* MA: *cohors II Nerviorum quingenaria cR* (RIB 1683) Co: *cohors II Pannoniorum quingenaria* (RIB 2411.143)	Ca: *cohors IIII Gallorum quingenaria eq* (RIB 1684, 1705) SA: *cohors IIII Gallorum quingenaria eq* (RIB 1686, 1706) P: *cohors IIII Gallorum quingenaria eq* (RIB 1710)
Carvoran I (*Magnis*)	3.70 (1.50)	H: *cohors I Hamiorum sagittariorum quingenaria* (RIB 1778)	See Carvoran II
Carlisle (*Luguvalium*)		MA: *ala Augusta quingenaria ob virtutem appellata* (RIB 946)	Ca: *vexillationes of legiones II Augusta & XX Valeria Victrix* (RIB 964.A, 965.B) *ala Gallorum Sebosiana quingenaria*

Outpost

Risingham (*Habitancum*)	4.10 (1.66)	MA: *cohors IIII Gallorum quingenaria eq* (RIB 1227, 1249)	SS: *cohors I Vangionum milliaria eq* (RIB 1234) Ca: *cohors I Vangionum milliaria eq* with *numeri Raeti gaesati & exploratores Habitancenses* (RIB 1235)
High Rochester (*Bremenium*)	5.10 (2.07)	AP: *cohors I Lingonum quingenaria eq* (RIB 1276) MA: *vexillationes of cohors IIII Gallorum quingenaria eq & cohors II Nerviorum quingenaria cR* (Britannia 1983, 337.12)	Ca: *cohors I fida Vardullorum milliaria eq cR* (RIB 1279) E: *cohors I fida Vardullorum milliaria eq cR* (RIB 1272, 1280) SA: *cohors I fida Vardullorum milliaria eq cR* (RIB 1281) Go: *cohors I fida Vardullorum milliaria eq cR* with *numerus exploratorum Bremeniensium* (RIB 1262)

Bewcastle (*Fanum Cocidii*)	6.30 (2.55)	H: *cohors I Aelia Dacorum milliaria* (*RIB* 991)	
Netherby (*Castra Exploratorum*)		AP: *cohors I Nervana Germanorum milliaria eq* (*RIB* 966) MA: *cohors I Aelia Hispanorum milliaria eq* (*RIB* 968)	Ca: *cohors I Aelia Hispanorum milliaria eq* (*RIB* 976-7, 980) SA: *cohors I Aelia Hispanorum milliaria eq* (*RIB* 978-9)
Birrens (*Blatovulgium*)	4.20 (1.70)	H: *cohors I Nervana Germanorum milliaria eq* (*RIB* 2093, 2097, 2116.B) AP: *cohors II Tungrorum milliaria eq cl* (*RIB* 2092, 2094, 2100, 2104, 2107-10)	Abandoned

Abbreviations

H = under Hadrian (r. AD 117–138)

AP = under Antoninus Pius (r. AD 138–161)

MA = under Marcus Aurelius (r. AD 161–180)

Co = under Commodus (r. AD 180–192)

SS = under Septimius Severus (r. AD 193–211)

Ca = under Caracalla (r. AD 211–217)

E = under Elagabalus (r. AD 218–222)

SA = under Severus Alexander (r. AD 222–235)

MT = under Maximinus Thrax (r. AD 235–238)

Go = under Gordian I, II or III (r. AD 238–244)

Ga = under Gallienus (r. AD 253–268)

A = under Aurelian (r. AD 270–275)

P = under Probus (r. AD 276–282)

cl = *coram laudata*

cR = *civium Romanorum*

pf = *pia fidelis*

eq = *equitata*

BELOW The latrine-block in the south-east corner of Housesteads fort (*Vercovicium*), with a drainage trench beneath the former seats, and a shallow channel at foot level and two stone basins for washing. There was no provision for individual privacy, Roman latrines were communal like their bathhouses. (Author's Collection)

In theory a fort's plan should provide clues to the type and size of auxiliary unit providing the garrison. Counting the number of barrack-blocks should allow the garrison size to be measured and possibly the type of auxiliary unit identified. Surprisingly, archaeology has shown that the neat one unit one fort arrangement was not necessarily adhered to. The identity of many of the original garrisons of the Wall-forts is therefore unknown, but most of the third-century garrisons are known from inscriptions and these probably represent a balance of forces similar to that in the second century.

The evidence from inscriptions and other sources presented for the positioning of the various auxiliary units covers those along the Wall itself, those on the Cumbrian coast, in the Stanegate forts and the northern outpost forts. References are selective, with preference being given to those inscriptions that are dated, unless these are not available. Thus in some cases the assignment of a unit's period of garrison to the time of a particular emperor is on the grounds of inherent probability rather than on the basis of a dated inscription. For instance, a unit may build or repair a fort, members of it may make a dedication, but the unit may not be in the garrison. Lead seals bearing unit names found at forts only apply to goods shipped by the unit, perhaps from elsewhere, and are not evidence for those units being stationed there and are therefore not treated as such. On the other hand, *diplomata* give lists of units and are dated, so they at least demonstrate the presence of the unit in Britain at a given date. Likewise the *Notitia Dignitatum*, a list of all known forces in the western half of the Roman Empire dated to the turn of the fifth century, shows units then in garrison at named forts, some of which can be identified. Many units first attested in the early third century were still in the same forts at the time of the *Notitia Dignitatum*.

Cavalry were present in strength, with an *ala milliaria* (the only unit of that size in Britannia) at Stanwix, and two *alae quingenariae* in forts along the eastern sector of the Wall, namely Benwell and Chesters. In addition there were

The latrine inside the reconstructed bathhouse at Wallsend fort (*Segedunum*) – note the key-shaped holes cut out of the stone-seats. (Author's Collection)

alae at Old Carlisle and Chester-le-Street, all within easy reach of Hadrian's Wall. These units, which represented five of the 18 *alae* known to be in Britain, were placed as near as possible to the two main roads running north of Hadrian's Wall, namely Dere Street passing through the Wall at the Portgate near Corbridge, and the road up Annandale crossing the Wall at Stanwix.

The three *cohortes peditatae*, on the other hand, were placed in the central sector furthest from these two roads, at Housesteads, Greatchesters and Birdoswald. The remaining garrisons were *cohortes equitata*. The temptation to speak of the horse element of a *cohors equitata* as mounted infantry must be avoided. On the march and in battle they were grouped with the *alae*. As they did not fight with their cohort they were classed as cavalry, though second-line cavalry in comparison to the *alae*, and for units stationed on the frontier they provided extended range for police and patrol work.

As there are only seven attested *cohortes milliariae* in Britain it is important to note that they tend to be all stationed in the Wall zone, perhaps compensating for the absence of the distant legions. Moreover, five of these seven were *equitatae*. The *quingenariae* units, on the other hand, seem rarely to have been in the Wall-zone in both the second and third centuries. Thus around half of the 49 *cohortes quingenariae* attested in Britain found themselves on the Wall at one time or another, in contrast with only one-quarter of the *alae*. Nevertheless, 18 of the 49 were *equitatae*, and about half of these saw service in the Wall-zone.

LEFT **A punitive raid against a Caledonii settlement** Although a spectacular imperial monument, Hadrian's Wall was not an impregnable obstacle. Besides, the Roman army was essentially an offensive, not a defensive, army. The reconstructed scene shows a punitive raid against a Caledonii settlement mounted by *cohors IIII Gallorum quingenaria equitata*. This part-mounted auxiliary unit garrisoned the northern outpost forts of Risingham and High Rochester during the reign of Marcus Aurelius (AD 161–180). Scenes (XX, XLVI, XCVIII, CII) from the Column of Marcus Aurelius in Rome, vividly depict auxiliaries ravaging and torching Macromanni settlements during the trans-Danubian campaigns of Marcus Aurelius (AD 171–173). Males capable of bearing arms are butchered, and women and children dragged off into captivity. We have, perhaps, a too favourable view of the Roman army and the nature of the Roman peace it enforced. In a pre-battle harangue, Calgacus, one of the Caledonii leaders who faced the Romans at Mons Graupius (AD 83), says, 'plunder, butcher, rapine, these things they misname empire: they make a desolation and call it peace' (Tacitus *Agricola* 30.5).

Life on Hadrian's Wall

Military documents, especially those from Egypt, Libya and Doura-Europos (a frontier fort on the Euphrates) tell us that the Roman army produced no end of paperwork. Their value for illustrating the minutiae of the internal workings of the army is immense. However, there are also unofficial documents that allow us a 'soldier's-eye view' of life on the frontiers. It is difficult to generalise about what life was like for the ordinary soldier, as conditions would certainly have varied between units and locations. Nevertheless, soldiers maintained contact with home and wrote and received letters that illuminate the more temporal side of army life:

> I have sent you ... pair of socks. From Sattua two pairs of sandals and two pairs of underpants, two pairs of sandals ... Greet ...ndes, Elpis, Iu..., ...enus, Tetricus and all your messmates (*contubernales*) with whom I hope that you live in the greatest of good fortune. (*Tab. Vindol.* II 346)

Written in colloquial Latin, this letter was evidently sent to a soldier serving at Chesterholm as the author refers to his messmates, one of whom, Elpis, bears a Greek name (lit. 'Hope'). The recipient was probably a member of one of three auxiliary cohorts known to have been stationed here in at the end of the first century, that is either *cohors III Batavorum*, *cohors VIIII Batavorum*, or *cohors I Tungrorum*. The writer also mentions various items of clothing and it seems probable that he or she is a close relative or friend whose concern for the recipient's material comfort led him or her to send a packet from home. Even if socks and underpants were not standard issue, provision of goods of this kind is abundantly paralleled in the papyri from Egypt, which thus indicates that they were worn as additional clothing. Finally, it is interesting to note that the Chesterholm texts shows us how swiftly auxiliary soldiers acquired literate habits and how proficient they became in Latin, a language that was not their own, but one that their military service forced them to acquire.

The extant private letters of Roman soldiers reveal a love-hate relationship with the army. They not only record their particular assignments or avoidance

The west gateway at Chesters fort (*Cilurnum*). Chesters projected north of the Wall, so this gateway is on the north side of the curtain-wall, which is running west in the left foreground. (Author's Collection)

of duties, but also promotions, hopes, fears, and illnesses. In addition, they also record concerns for family, generosity with money or impecunious requests for cash, food and equipment, personal business and financial transactions. These letters give the distinct impression, that once a soldier had finished his daily duties, he had considerable personal freedom. The thoughts of auxiliary soldiers in an isolated outpost on the road from Koptos in Egypt to the Red Sea were almost exclusively of food (*CPL* 303–7, *SB* 9017), although a few had 'camp wives' to relieve the boredom (*P. Mich.* 8, 9).

Duties

A soldier's duties were recorded on a daily basis. In the daily report of the unit, which gave the unit's muster strength, the soldier would be marked as present and correct. Besides training, parades and inspections, there were routine duties, including mounting guard at the *principia*, at the granary, and at the gateways, cleaning centurions' kit, latrine and bathhouse fatigues, and sweeping the camp. The duty rosters of *cohors XX Palmyrenorum milliaria equitata*, stationed at Doura-Europos during the first half of the third century, show that up to 25 per cent of the unit was detailed daily to guard-duties (*RMR* 12–19). The soldier also had to clean his own kit, weapons and armour, collect fuel for his own cooking, and gather fodder for the camp animals. If he varied the tedium of fort life by being assigned to a party going out for supplies, or on escort duty, or on secondment to another unit, his absence would be recorded, and his return if his absence was for more than one day.

An extant strength report of *cohors I Tungrorum* from Chesterholm, dated to *c.* AD 90, illustrates this point superbly (*Tab. Vindol.* II 154). It shows a much-reduced garrison, with 296 men present, including 31 unfit for active service, and 456 absent. Of the latter, 337 were at Corbridge, 46 detached for service as guards with the provincial governor, one centurion in London, and detachments, of six, nine, 11 and 45 men respectively, at four other locations that are not legible. The total strength of the unit, 752 men, is close enough to the complement of 800, the nominal size of a *cohors milliaria peditata*.

Diet

It is a remarkable fact that even during the rare mutinies there are no recorded complaints about the Roman military diet, and it appears that the average soldier ate better than or at least as well as many civilians of a similar social

The pillared floor-supports and loading platform of the north granary at Housesteads fort (*Vercovicium*). The pillars once supported a flagged floor to be seen at Corbridge and Birdoswald. (Author's Collection)

background. Even the *auxilia* stationed in frontier forts had a well-balanced and varied diet. The basic rations carried in the field were bacon-lard, hardtack, salt, sour wine and wheat, the latter being milled by the soldier himself and then made into unleavened bread, porridge or pasta. Meat and cheese were eaten when available. The diet in the fort was still based on wheat, though it could be varied, as animals were kept on land assigned to the fort, requisitioned, bought or hunted. Milk and cheese could again be obtained from the unit's own herds, requisitioned or purchased. A variety of local fruit and vegetables were also eaten.

Analysis of the sewage at Bearsden on the Antonine Wall has confirmed that the military diet was high in fibre and mainly vegetarian, although documentary and archaeological evidence does demonstrate that meat was also consumed. The sewage from the fort contained fragments of wheat, barley, bean, fig, dill, coriander, opium poppy (possibly used on bread as today), hazelnut, raspberry, bramble, strawberry, bilberry, and celery. Fig, dill, coriander and celery, the seeds of which were used medicinally, were imported from the Mediterranean. The sewage also tells us that the soldiers suffered from whipworm and roundworm, and some of their grain appears to have been contaminated with weevils. An excellent picture of the meat soldiers ate can be seen from the analysis of animal bones from forts in Britain and Germany. Ox, sheep and pig were most popular, but goat, red and roe deer, wild boar, hare, fowl both domesticated and wild, fish and shellfish were also eaten. Other fruits consumed included apples, pears, plums, cherries, peaches, grapes, elderberries, damsons, apricots, olives, and pomegranates, as well as nuts such

Detail of an under-floor ventilator with central mullion at the west granary of Corbridge (*Coria*). This ventilator allowed air to circulate under the floor and thus protect foodstuffs from becoming damp. (Author's Collection)

as sweet chestnuts, walnuts, and beechnuts. The Chesterholm-*Vindolanda* writing-tablets refer to a wide range of vegetables, including cabbage, garden peas, broad beans and horse beans, carrots, radishes, and garlic, not to mention pulses such as lentils and chickpeas. Eggs should not be forgotten, nor salt, spices and vinegar. Wines of varying vintage and Celtic beer are also mentioned. To sweeten their food soldiers used honey, and, like all Romans they were fond of using fish sauces (*muria*), somewhat akin to present-day Thai or Vietnamese fish sauce, to flavour their food. Besides being mentioned in surviving texts, *muria* was once stored in one of the amphorae unearthed at Chesterholm.

Normally two square meals were eaten each day, what we would call lunch (*prandium*) and supper (*cena*). In theory each soldier was provided with a daily ration of food, which he cooked himself as there were no central cookhouses. The Carvoran grain-measure (*modius*) from the Stanegate fort of the same name, however, holds the equivalent of seven daily rations (*c.* 9.82 litres up to the gauge mark) and suggests that the grain was given out weekly (*RIB* 2415.56). Moreover, as each soldier slept eight to a room or tent, we can assume that they pooled their food with one man taking on the cooking for the group. This is supported by the discovery of cooking implements and millstones marked with the name of barrack-room groups (*contubernia*), whilst in the Chesterholm-*Vindolanda* writing-tablets we read of references to a soldier's 'messmates'. Josephus (*Bellum Iudaicum* 3.85) implies that food was eaten communally by *contubernia*, whilst Appian (*Iberica* 85) states that the two standard ways of cooking were roasting and boiling, and along with a mess-tin each soldier had a camp-kettle and a roasting-spit as standard issue.

Alcohol

Several literary sources (Appian *Iberica* 54, *SHA*, Hadrian 10.2, Vegetius 3.3) speak of the iron rations a soldier carried when on active service, which included *acetum*, a sour wine, at times mixed with water to form a drink called *posca*.

From the graffiti on wine amphorae found on military sites we also have an indication that the soldier drank more than just *acetum*. The best collection comes from the first-century legionary fortress at *Vindonissa* (Windisch), Germania Superior. Here examples have been discovered mentioning 'very mature' wine from Surrento in southern Italy, wine from Messina in Sicily, and a third old wine is also recorded, perhaps a form of fruit cocktail of wine infused on fruit. Wine was also imported from southern Gaul and the Iberian peninsula. Further information is provided by graffiti on amphorae discovered in Britain. One written in ink, on the neck of an amphora found in the wine cellar of the supply depot at Richborough, mentions wine from Mount Vesuvius. An

Buttresses of the north granary at Housesteads fort (*Vercovicium*), a common feature of a stone-built granary with its broad roof and wide eaves-drip. There is an under-floor ventilator positioned centrally. (Author's Collection)

amphora from Newstead had the word *vinum* ('vintage wine') scratched on the handle to identify its contents and graffiti on amphorae from Mumrills and Wallsend record 'sweet wine' and 'honey sweetened wine' respectively.

Clearly beer (*cervesa*) was also popular with the troops, especially so when you consider the Celtic or Germanic origins of those serving in the *auxilia*. An inscription (*AE* 1928.183) mentions a discharged soldier of the *classis Germanica* who had set himself up in the late first century to supply local beer to the military market in Germania Inferior. A number of military sites in northern Britain have shown evidence for the widespread use of barley. This grain may have been animal feed or punishment rations as literary sources suggest (Suetonius *Divus Augustus* 24.2, Frontinus *Strategemata* 4.1.25, 37, Plutarch *Antony* 39.7, Vegetius 1.13, cf. Polybius 6.38.3). Alternatively, there could have been a demand for large quantities of beer, for which barley would have been used, as can be seen from several of the Chesterholm-*Vindolanda* writing-tablets. One of them (*Tab. Vindol.* II 190) records the procurement, for a week, of over 46 litres of wine including Massic, an Italian vintage of high reputation, some sour wine, and 69 litres of Celtic beer, along with 187 litres of barley (*hordeum*). Another letter (*Tab. Vindol.* II 343) refers to some 1,715 litres of threshed *bracis*, another cereal known to have been used in the production of Celtic beer. That the brewing itself might well have been done at or near Chesterholm is strongly suggested by a reference to a *cervasarius* (brewer) named Atrectus (*Tab. Vindol.* II 182). This thirst for beer is epitomised in a postscript to a letter written by the decurion Masclus to his commander the prefect Flavius Cerialis, adding, 'the comrades have no beer, which I ask that you order to be sent' (Inv. 93/1544, cf. 93/1495). Having been detailed to collect winter wheat for the garrison, perhaps from Corbridge, Masclus and his men were thus absent from the fort and obviously missing their creature comforts.

Bathing

Whilst it was customary to build legionary baths inside the fortress, those of the auxiliaries were normally sited outside the fort. The bathhouses of Hadrian's Wall show a standard plan. They were four- or five-roomed stone structures of the block type comprising the basic cold (*frigidarium*), warm (*tepidarium*), and hot (*caldarium*) rooms, with a latrine attached. The bather entered the cold room first, then proceeded through rooms of increasingly higher temperatures, thereafter retracing his steps to the cold room, where water splashed over the body served to close up the pores before the bather dressed and came out again

The bathhouse at Chesters fort (*Cilurnum*), looking west, with the latrine in the foreground and the *apodyterium* in the background. Of particular interest are the niches that once housed timber clothes-lockers. (Author's Collection)

into the open air. The floors were raised off the ground on a sequence of small pillars or brick stacks, the hypocaust system of under-floor heating, and heat supplied from one or more furnaces. Heat was also carried up the walls in sets of square-sectioned clay pipes or box-flues.

A military bathhouse was much more than places to sweat out the dirt. In a very real sense it was the Roman soldiers' equivalent of the NAAFI in the British Army. The excavation reports from bathhouses in northern Britain show that troops relaxed in the heated changing rooms (*apodyteria*) with mugs of imported wine or local Celtic beer, played dice or board games and, since Roman soldiers were partial to shellfish, nibbled delicacies such as mussels and oysters. On the northern frontier supplies of mussels and oysters are recorded at Bar Hill, Benwell, Chesters, Corbridge, High Rochester, Maryport, Mumrills, Newstead, Rudchester and South Shields. Oysters were discovered stored in the wine cellar at Richborough, and Juvenal refers to oysters 'bred on the beds of Richborough' (4.140, cf. Pliny *Naturalis historia* 9.169), which suggests the army in Britannia had its own source for shellfish. That they gambled is certain. An altar was found at the south wall of the *apodyterium* (changing room) of the bathhouse inside the Antonine Wall fort of Balmuildy dedicated by Caecilius Nepos, a tribune of an unnamed auxiliary unit, to Fortuna, the genius of such matters (*RIB* 2189). Nearby were scattered counters and parts of a gaming-board.

Gaming

Parts of a ceramic gaming-board, consisting of two rows of roughly incised heart-shaped ivy-leaves divided by a geometric pattern down the centre, were found at the works depot of *legio XX Valeria Victrix* at Holt. Along with this board were found three dice. The board was probably used for *duodecim scripta* ('twelve points'). This was an early form of backgammon played between two persons on a board of three-by-twelve points, each player had 15 counters whose moves were governed by the throws of three dice. Ovid, an Augustan poet, describes it as 'a sort of game confined by subtle method into as many lines as the slippery year has months' (*Ars amatoria* 3.363–5), whilst Ausonius, in praising the late fourth-century AD orator Minervius for his memory, says of this game:

Gaming-board and counters, on display in the museum at Wallsend fort. Off duty pastimes included, then as now, games of chance. (Author's Collection)

Once after a long contested game, I have seen you tell over all the throws made by either side when the dice were tipped out with a sharp spin over the fillets cut out in the hollowed boxwood of the dice-box; and recount move by move, without mistake, which pieces had been lost, which won back, through the long stretches of the game. (*Commemoratio professorium Burdigalensiun* 1.25)

The counters were generally bone roundels, mostly coloured black and white or blue and white, although occasionally coloured stone or glass pieces were used. On some surviving gaming-boards letters mark the points for the pieces. It is possible that these boards belong to a modified version of *duodecim scripta*, the problem, however, is that they contain neither 12 markings nor 12 letters, but 36 letters or squares. Whatever, the marvellous thing about these boards it that the letters tend to spell out clever sentences. Mostly these sentences relate to gambling and good fortune, or matters with military overtones, thus indicating the probable use of these boards by soldiers.

Another popular game with the soldiers was *ludus latrunculorum* ('robber-soldiers') a battle-game in which pieces could be moved like the rook in a game of chess. *Ludus latrunculorum* is first specifically mentioned by the first-century BC author Varro (*De lingua Latina* 10.22), but almost certainly derives from the Greek game *petteia* ('pebbles'), which Plato (*Phaedrus* 274d) tells us originally came from Egypt. The Greek rhetorician Pollux of Naucratis, who flourished during the reign of Commodus, describes the game as follows::

The game played with many pieces is a board with spaces disposed among lines. The board is called the 'city' and each piece is called a 'dog'; the pieces are of two colours, and the art of the game consists in taking a piece of one colour by enclosing it between two of the other colour. (*Onomasticon* 98)

Likewise, Ovid (*Ars amatoria* 3.358–9, *Tristia* 2.477–82, cf. Martial 14.17) tells us that pieces were taken in *ludus latrunculorum* by being surrounded by two enemy pieces in rank or file, and that backward moves were also permitted. Stone (sometimes precious) or glass playing pieces of different colours (Ovid *Ars amatoria* 2.208, *Tristia* 2.477, Martial 14.18) were deployed on boards with varying numbers of squares, but eight-by-eight seems to have been the most

Loading platform, portico columns and drainage channel from the west granary at Corbridge (*Coria*). The double-doors opened onto the sheltered platform up to which carts could be brought for unloading. (Author's Collection)

common. The number of playing pieces found with them also varies. The implication from Martial (7.72.8, cf. 5.23.7, Juvenal 3.237) is that there were a lot of them as he uses the term *mandra*, which could be taken as meaning a 'drove' of pieces on the board.

In Britain these boards survive, cut on stone, from the fortress at Chester, the forts of Newstead, Birdoswald, Corbridge and Wallsend, from milecastles 40 (Winshields) and 50 (High House) and turret 52a (Banks East), and the supply depot at Richborough. The player who succeeded in removing the most pieces won the game (cf. Seneca *Dialogi* 9.14.7), and according to Vopiscus (13.2) the victor was hailed *imperator*, another indication of the military aspect of the game. There is an elaborate and obscure account of the game in the poem known as *Laus Pisonis* (cf. Tacitus *Annales* 15.48):

> Cunningly the pieces are disposed on the open board, and battles are fought with soldiery of glass, so that now white blocks black, now black blocks white. But every foe yields to you, Piso: marshalled by you, what piece ever gave way? What piece on the brink of death dealt not death to his enemy? Thousandfold are your battle-tactics: one man in fleeing from an attacker himself overpowers him. Another, who has been standing on the lookout, comes up from a distant point of vantage. Another stoutly rushes into mêlée, and cheats his foe now creeping on his prey. Another courts blockade on either flank, and, under feint of being blocked, he blocks two men. Another's objective is more ambitious, that he may quickly break through the massed phalanx, swoop into the lines, and razing the enemy's rampart do havoc in the walled stronghold. Meanwhile, although the fight rages fiercely now the hostile ranks are spilt, yet you yourself are victorious with serried line unbroken, or despoiled may be one or two men, and both your hands rattle with the imprisoned throng. (*Laus Pisonis* 192–208)

It appears the best tactic consists in massing your pieces in a phalanx. However, when the enemy has succeeded, through skilful play and a certain amount of sacrifice to himself, in breaking through that phalanx, he has free room to manoeuvre in its rear and cause havoc. The game is last mentioned by Macrobius (*fl. c.* AD 400), when he rebukes those that 'played at *tabula* and *latrunculi*' (*Saturnalia* 1.5).

Claudius, according to Suetonius (*Divus Claudius* 33.2), was a fervent devotee of dice, so much so that he wrote a history on the subject. Moreover, he used to play while out driving, on a board fitted to his carriage that kept the dice from rolling off capriciously. Emperors aside, playing dice (*tesserae*) was an extremely popular game among soldiers. A pair of bone dice found at Birdoswald fort, each of whose sides has a different number of ring-and-dot markings (1 to 6), were no different from their modern counterparts. Yet the Romans did have a type with only four marked faces called *tali*, examples of which again come from Birdoswald. These antler dice have four flat faces marked 1, 3, 4 and 6, while the remaining two sides are rounded and blank. In a game of *tali* four such dice were thrown. According to Ovid (*Tristia* 2.4.73–4, cf. Martial 14.14), the highest throw was the 'Venus' (1, 3, 4, 6), the lowest the 'Dogs' (four aces). In a version played by Augustus any player throwing the 'Dogs' or a *senio* ('six') put four *denarii* into the pool, which was scooped by the first player to throw the 'Venus' (Suetonius *Divus Augustus* 71.2).

Whether with four or six marked faces, dice were shaken in a cup and then tossed, as is clearly demonstrated in a fresco from an inn at Pompeii (Naples Museum, inv. 111482). In a military context, examples made of bone or antler have been found at many sites including Richborough, Great Chesterford, Wroxeter, Newstead and Wallsend, and the dice are not always true as show by the 'loaded' dice from Housesteads. Associated with the game of dice are marked gambling chips. These chips, which are generally made of bone, carry numerical markings on one side. The most common markings are X, V, and I, with only a small proportion marked with other numerals. Many of the chips marked with X have an extra vertical line through the middle, which symbolises one *denarius*. Some of the chips are even labelled *remittam libenter* ('I will gladly repay'), which brings to mind Juvenal's remark that nowadays men came to 'the hazard of the gaming table armed not with purses but with a treasure-chest'. (1.90)

Sports

The father of Valentinian I (r. AD 364–375), the elder Gratian, was famed for his great physical strength and skill at wrestling in the soldiers' fashion. He was, as Ammianus Marcellinus aptly puts it, 'a second Milo of Croton' (30.7.2–3). Tacitus records that one inter-services wrestling competition between a legionary and a Gallic auxiliary attracted a large crowd. However, the excessively partisan spirit displayed by the rival supporters spoiled the match:

> Thus it happened that two soldiers – one belonging to *legio V Alaudae*, πthe other a Gallic auxiliary – were induced by high spirits to engage in a bout of wrestling. The legionary took a fall, and the Gaul jeered at his discomfited opponent. Thereupon the spectators who had gathered round took sides, the legionaries set about the auxiliaries, and two cohorts were annihilated. (*Historiae* 2.68)

Other popular forms of blood sports, for those who could afford it, included hunting. As a youth undergoing his military training, Hadrian aroused criticism because of his passion for hunting (*SHA, Hadrian* 2.1). The wilder frontiers of the empire provided ample opportunity for such pursuits. In Britannia wild boar roamed the Pennines along with wolves, deer and foxes. Gaius Tetius Veturius Micianus, prefect of *ala Gallorum Sebosiana* stationed at Binchester, dedicated an altar to 'Silvanus the unconquered' for the capture of a wild boar of remarkable fine appearance who had escaped his predecessors (*RIB* 1041). No doubt he employed some of his troopers as beaters.

At times the military authorities arranged entertainment for the troops, such as gladiatorial and animal displays. Although the literary references are somewhat vague here (Tacitus *Annales* 1.22, 13.31), the archaeological record attests to

The hospital at Housesteads fort (*Vercovicium*) – note the paved courtyard and the long room at the north end, which probably served as an operating theatre. (Author's Collection)

amphitheatres being very much a part of garrison life. At Chester, for example, the amphitheatre outside the fortress could accommodate 7,000 spectators and clearly served the legion as well as most of the non-military population in the nearby *canabae*.

Women

From the reign of Augustus to that of Septimius Severus a serving soldier, whether citizen or non-citizen, was not allowed to contract a legal marriage (Dio 60.24.3, Herodian 3.8.5). It is not clear what the significance of this was to their daily life since there were a number of different forms of marital status in the Roman world and, as in pre-modern rural Britain, marital ties were often fairly informal. The crucial question concerned the inheritance of Roman citizenship by the soldiers' children; hence the importance given to the *diplomata*. However, leaving legal niceties to one side, a man signed up for at least 25 years, the best years of his life, and thus to him the solution was obvious. If he could not be married officially, he would marry unofficially. Nevertheless, marriage was not the only reason that a soldier coveted a woman's company.

Graffiti from Doura-Europos tells us of an *optio* who seems to have been responsible for billeting a troupe of mimes and actresses, the former providing dramatic, the latter more personal entertainment in what was virtually a camp brothel. A large tavern and brothel complex in the *canabae* at *Carnuntum* (Petronell), Pannonia Superior, served the more basic needs and desires of the nearby legionary fortress. Graffiti in brothels at Pompeii record the visits of off-duty soldiers: 'Caius Valerius Venustus, soldier of the first cohort' reads one (*CIL* 4.2145, cf. 2157). It seems there were always women whom a soldier could visit when his desire was too much to bear, or when his feelings rebelled against the unremitting company of other men.

Leave

According to Velleius Paterculus (2.95.1), a former *praefectus alae* under Augustus, and Vegetius (2.19, 3.4, 26) it was military policy to ensure that the troops did not receive too much free time (*otium*). What mattered to a Roman commander was that his men could fight efficiently and defeat an enemy. There was a certain concern for their welfare as the provision of garrison bathhouses and hospitals proves, but all else was irrelevant. Of course, in theory, an army may be more efficient if its serving members are teetotal and celibate, and wedded only to the idea of discipline. Hence leave was not on the job description of the Roman soldier, and Suetonius (*Galba* 6.3) imparts that Galba, as governor of Germania Superior, came down hard on those who requested leave. However, it was granted as papyrus documents and Chesterholm-*Vindolanda* writing-tablets bear witness to the formal applications to commanding officers for leave (*commeatus*). 'Am I going to get a furlough?' was 78th in a list of standard questions put to an oracle in Egypt (*P. Oxy.* 1447.78). A duty roster of *legio III Cyrenaica*, covering the first ten days of October AD 87, shows two legionaries enjoying their leave (*RMR* 9). On the other hand, a duty roster of *cohors XX Palmyrenorum*, dated to AD 219, shows two soldiers failing to return from leave (*RMR* 1). How long soldiers were granted is not known, nor where most of them went, but perhaps the nearest large town might offer most scope for the bearer of a leave-pass as is suggested by the request for leave from a soldier serving at Chesterholm to visit nearby Corbridge (*Tab. Vindol.* II 175).

Soldier and civilian

In their ideal role the troops, in the words of Dio of Prusa (1.28), were like shepherds who, with the emperor, guarded the flock of the empire. Of course, some communities did benefit from the proximity of garrisons. But the dominating theme in the sources is the brutal oppression of civilians by soldiers. Juvenal (16.24–5), the satirist who once commanded *cohors I Delmatarum* in Britannia, vividly depicts how the unfortunate pedestrian might have his foot crushed by a soldier's hobnailed boot in the crush of the streets. He also spoke of beatings and intimidation for which redress was hard to find. An encounter with an off-duty soldier could be a frightening experience. In Petronius' bawdy novel *Satyricon*, written probably during the reign of Nero (AD 54–68), the hero rushes into the street with his hand on his sword hilt:

> Then a soldier spotted me; he was probably a deserter or a nocturnal cutthroat. 'Hey comrade', he said, 'what legion or whose century do you belong to?' I lied boldly about my legion and century, but he said: 'Well then, in your army do soldiers walk about wearing white slippers?' Since my expression and my trembling gave away that I had been lying, he ordered me to hand over my sword and to watch out for myself. So, I was robbed. (*Satyricon* 82)

Official documents from Egypt containing the complaints of civilians preserve an authentic record of widespread abuse, not only through robbery but also extortion (*SB* 9207, *SP* 221, *P. Oxy.* 240). The attraction for the civilians, however, was the regular pay of the soldier (basic auxiliary pay was nearly five-sixths that of a legionary, who received 300 *denarii* per annum). Because they needed the profit derived from filling the soldier's belly, slaking his thirst and satisfying his lusts, they were exposed to his unruly behaviour.

Of course there were always the delights of the *vici* that clustered around the forts. A short step away, these had much to offer the bored soldier with a little money in his pouch, so much so that Hadrian, who was imposing a tighter discipline on the army, had to limit the number of inns and eating houses outside military establishments. He also reined in what appears to be the practice amongst troops to be absent without leave (*SHA, Hadrian* 10.3). Fronto (*Principia Historiae* 12) says that the army in Syria spent more time in the nearby beer-gardens and theatres than in camp, and as a consequence the soldiers were frequently drunk and wont to gamble. Indeed, the garrison of Syria had a long

A cavalry barrack-block at Chesters fort (*Cilurnum*) with the spacious quarters for the *decurio* in the foreground. A drainage channel runs down the street separating two barrack-blocks. (Author's Collection)

history of not being disciplined. In AD 57 Gnaeus Domitius Corbulo had gone there to conduct a war against the Parthians only to find his new command was made up, in the cutting words of Tacitus, of 'flashy money-makers who had soldiered in towns' (*Annales* 13.35). He quickly remedied the situation by taking the badly under-exercised army up into the inhospitable highlands of Armenia around Lake Van, where they built camps and went on manoeuvres. Nine years later, however, Vespasian was to be met with exactly the same problem and his Syrian command had to be licked into shape through old-school discipline (Suetonius *Divus Vespasianus* 4.6).

Excavations in the Hadrian's Wall *vici* show plenty of evidence for shops, inns and gambling establishments where the soldiers could, in Severus Alexander's words, 'make love, drink, wash' (*SHA, Severus Alexander* 53). Perhaps not quite the 'roaring, rioting, cock-fighting, wolf-baiting, horse-riding town' as colourfully painted by Centurion Parnesius in Kipling's *Puck of Pook's Hill*, a *vicus* did, nonetheless, serve as a conveniently close location for the soldiers to let off steam and thus satisfy their basic needs and urges. Here they could gamble and drink. More importantly, here they could meet with local women, whether they were called wives, mistresses, or prostitutes, who having formed liaisons with soldiers often bore their children. An inscription (*ILS* 2304) from near Alexandria and dated to AD 194, records the names of 46 soldiers who had just received their honourable discharge from *legio II Traiana fortis*. Of the 41 whose origins were mentioned, 32 were from Egypt, and 24 stated the military camp as their birthplace (*origo castris*). It is likely that most of them were illegitimate sons born to soldiers from local women.

The sites today

Today there is no more potent symbol of the Roman army than the remains of Hadrian's Wall. Numerous stretches of the Wall and its related fortifications are still visible along its original line from Bowness-on-Solway, Cumbria, in the west, to Wallsend, Tyneside, in the east. Of particular interest are the Wall-forts of Chesters and Housesteads, and the nearby site of Corbridge, all of which are under the guardianship of English Heritage. Other forts can be visited at South Shields, Wallsend, Chesterholm and Birdoswald. Museum collections can be seen at the Museum of Antiquities, University of Newcastle upon Tyne, Tullie House Museum, Carlisle, Senhouse Roman Museum, Maryport, as well as the on-site museums at South Shields, Wallsend, Chesters, Corbridge, Housesteads and Chesterholm. There is also the Roman Army Museum at Carvoran and the reconstructed bathhouse at Wallsend. The best-preserved stretches of the curtain-wall lie between Chesters and Birdoswald, although some turrets are visible west of the latter fort and fragments of the Wall can be seen in the first 13 miles of its course through urban Tyneside.

Sites along Hadrian's Wall are well signposted and easily accessible from the A69 Carlisle to Newcastle road, and the 'Military Road' (B6318), which runs close to the Wall itself.

Useful contact information

Hadrian's Wall Information Line	01434 322002
Traveline	0870 608 2 608
National Rail Enquiries	08457 48 49 50
Hadrian's Wall Tourism Partnership	www.hadrian's-wall.org
Northumberland National Park Authority	www.nnpa.org.uk
Journey Planner	www.jplanner.org.uk
Traveline	www.traveline.org
English Heritage	www.english-heritage.org.uk

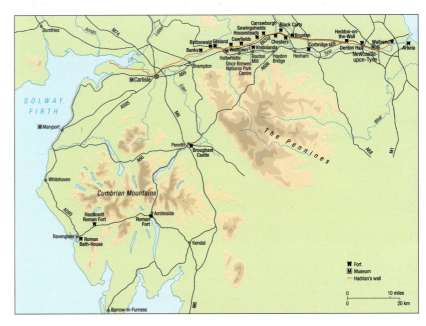

Major sites of interest and museums along the length of Hadrian's Wall. (© Copyright Osprey Publishing Limited)

Further reading and research

Bidwell, P. T., *Roman Forts in Britain*, Batsford/English Heritage, London, 1997

Bidwell, P. T. (ed.), *Hadrian's Wall 1989–1999: A Summary of Recent Excavation and Research*, Cumberland and Westmorland Antiquarian Society and Society of Antiquaries of Newcastle Upon Tyne, Carlisle, 1999

Birley, A. R., 'A new tombstone from Vindolanda', *Britannia* 29, 299–306, London: Society for the Promotion of Roman Studies, 1998

Birley, A. R., *Hadrian: the Restless Emperor*, Routledge, London, 1998

Birley, R. E., *Vindolanda: A Roman Frontier Post on Hadrian's Wall*, Thames & Hudson, London, 1977

Birley, R. E., *Garrison Life on the Roman Frontier*, Roman Army Museum, Carvoran, 1991

Bowman, A. K., *The Roman Writing Tablets from Vindolanda*, British Museum, London, 1983

Bowman, A. K., *Life and Letters on the Roman Frontier*, British Museum, London, 1994

Bowman, A. K., and Thomas, J. D., *The Vindolanda Writing Tablets: Tabulae Vindolandenses II*, British Museum, London, 1994

Breeze, D. J., *The Northern Frontiers of Roman Britain*, Batsford, London, 1993

Breeze, D. J., *Roman Forts in Britain*, Shire, Princes Risborough, 1994

Breeze, D. J., *Hadrian's Wall Souvenir Guide*, English Heritage, London, 1996

Breeze, D. J., 'Regiments and frontiers: Patterns of distribution on rivers and artificial frontiers', W. Groenman-van Waateringe *et al.* (eds.), *Roman Frontier Studies 1995: Proceedings of the XVIth International Congress of Roman Frontier Studies*, 73–74, Oxbow, Oxford, 1997

Breeze, D. J., and Dobson, B., *Hadrian's Wall*, 4th edition, Penguin, London, 2000

Cheesman, G. L., *The Auxilia of the Roman Army*, Georg Olms, New York, 1971

Collingwood Bruce, J., *Handbook to the Roman Wall*, 13th edition, Harold Hill, Newcastle, 1978

Crow, J., *Housesteads*, Batsford/English Heritage, London, 1995

Davies, R. W., *Service in the Roman Army*, Edinburgh University Press, Edinburgh, 1989

De la Bédoyère, G., *Hadrian's Wall: History and Guide*, 2nd edition, Tempus, Stroud, 2001

De la Bédoyère, G., *Eagles over Britannia: The Roman Army in Britain*, Tempus, Stroud, 2001

Dobson, B., and Mann J. C., 'Roman army in Britain – Britons in Roman army', *Britannia* 4, 191–205, Society for the Promotion of Roman Studies, London, 1973

Goldsworthy, A. K., *The Roman Army at War, 100 BC–AD 200*, Clarendon Press, Oxford, 1998

Heywood, B., 'The Vallum – its problems restated', Jarrett, M. G., and Dobson, B. (eds.), *Britain and Rome: Essays Presented to Eric Birley on his Sixtieth Birthday*, 85–94, Titus Kendal, Wilson, 1965

Holder, P. A., *Studies in the Auxilia of the Roman Army from Augustus to Trajan*, BAR International Series 70, Oxford, 1980

Holder, P. A., *The Roman Army in Britain*, Batsford, London, 1982

Jarrett, M. G., 'Non-legionary troops in Roman Britain: part one, the units', *Britannia* 25, 35–77, Society for the Promotion of Roman Studies, London, 1994

Johnson, A., *Roman Forts*, Black, London, 1983

Johnson, S., *Hadrian's Wall*, Batsford/English Heritage, London, 2000

Kendal, R., 'Transport logistics associated with the building of Hadrian's Wall', *Britannia* 27, 129–152, Society for the Promotion of Roman Studies, London, 1996

Keppie, L. J. F., *The Making of the Roman Army*, Routledge, London, 1998

Le Bohec, Y., *The Imperial Roman Army*, Routledge, London, 2000

Lepper, F. and Frere, S. S., *Trajan's Column: A New Edition of the Chicorius Plates*, Sutton, Stroud, 1988

Saddington, D. B., 'The 'politics' of the *auxilia* and the forging of auxiliary regimental identity', Groenman-van Waateringe, W., *et al.* (eds.), *Roman Frontier Studies 1995: Proceedings of the XVIth International Congress of Roman Frontier Studies*, 493–496, Oxbow, Oxford, 1997

Shirley, E. A. M., *Building a Roman Legionary Fortress*, Stroud, Tempus, 2001

Shotter, D. C. A., *The Roman Frontier in Britain: Hadrian's Wall, the Antonine Wall and Roman Policy in the North*, Carnegie, Preston, 1996

Webster, G., *The Roman Imperial Army of the First and Second Centuries AD*, 3rd edition, Black, London, 1985

Wilmott, T., *Birdoswald Roman Fort: 1880 Years on Hadrian's Wall*, Tempus, Stroud, 2001

Glossary

The following provides much of the terminology associated with Roman fortifications of the first and second centuries and their garrisons. In most cases both singular and plural forms are given (i.e. singular/plural).

acetum Sour wine

acta diurna Daily orders

agger/aggeres Rampart

ala/alae Cavalry 'wing'

annona Rations

aquilifer Bearer of a legion's eagle-standard (*aquila*)

armilla/armillae Armlets – military decoration

as/asses Copper coin (equal to ¼ *sestertius*)

ascensus Stairway

aureus Gold coin (equal to 25 *denarii*)

ballistarium/ballistaria Platform for stone-thrower (*ballista*) or bolt-thrower (*catapulta*)

balneum/balnea Bathhouse

beneficiarius/beneficiarii Senior officer's aid

bipennis/bipenna Double-edged axe

buccellata Hardtack

bucinator/bucinatores Musician who blew the *bucina*, a horn used to regulate watches

burgus/burgi Watchtower

campus Parade ground

canabae Extramural settlement (fortress)

capitus Fodder

capsarius/capsarii Paramedic

cena Evening meal

centuria/centuriae 1. Cohort sub-unit 2. Barrack-block

centurio/centuriones *Centuria* or legionary cohort commander

cervesa Celtic beer

cervus/cervi Chevaux-de-frise

clava/clavae Wooden practise-sword

clavicula/claviculae Curved extension of rampart protecting a gateway

clibanus/clibani Bread-oven

cohors peditata/cohortes peditatae
1. Auxiliary cohort
cohors quingenaria peditata: 480 infantry (6 *centuriae*) under a *praefectus cohortis*
cohors milliaria peditata: 800 infantry (10 *centuriae*) under a *tribunus*
2. Legionary cohort, ten per legion
cohors prima: 800 legionaries (5 'double-strength' *centuriae*) under a *primus pilus*
cohortes II–X: each 480 legionaries (6 *centuriae*) under a *pilus prior*

cohors equitata/cohortes equitatae Mixed auxiliary cohort of foot and horse

contubernium/contubernia Mess-unit of eight infantry, ten per century

cornicen/cornicines Musician who blew the *cornu*, a horn associated with the standards

cornicularius/cornicularii Junior officer responsible for clerks in *principia*

corniculum/corniculi Horn-shaped military decoration – awarded for bravery

corona/coronae Crown – military decoration generally reserved for centurions and above
corona absidionalis: crown of grass – awarded for rescuing besieged army
corona aurea: gold crown – awarded for various exploits
corona civica: crown of oak leaves – awarded for saving life of a citizen
corona muralis: mural crown in gold – awarded to first man over walls of besieged town
corona vallaris: rampart crown in gold – awarded to first man over enemy's rampart

cratis/crates Wickerwork practice-shield

cuneus/cunei 'Wedge', i.e. irregular cavalry unit

curator/curatores *Turma* second-in-command

custos armorum Armourer

decurio/decuriones *Turma* commander

denarius/denarii Silver coin (= 4 *sestertii*)

deposita Soldiers' bank

diploma/diplomata Military discharge certificate

dolabra/dolabrae Pickaxe

dona militaria Military decorations

duplicarius Double-pay

dupondius/dupondii Brass coin (= 2 *asses*)

emeritus/emeriti Veteran

eques/equites Trooper

excubitor/excubitores Sentinel

explorator/exploratores Scout

fabrica/fabricae Workshop

fossa/fossae Ditch

frumentarius/frumentarii Intelligence officer

frumentum Wheat

honesta missio Honourable discharge

hordeum Barley

horreum/horrea Granary

imaginifer Bearer of the emperor's image (*imago*)

immunis/immunes Soldier exempt from fatigues

intervallum Open space between rear of rampart and built-up area

latera praetorii Central part of fort between *viae principalis* and *quintana*

lavatrina Latrine-block

legatus Augusti legionis *Legio* commander (senatorial rank)

legio/legiones Legion (5,120 men all ranks)

libra Roman pound (equal to *c.* 323 grams)

librarius/librarii Clerk
librarius horreorum: kept granary records
librarius depositorum: collected soldiers' savings
librarius caducorum: secured belongings of those killed in action

lilia Pits containing sharpened stakes (*cippi*)

lorica Breastwork

ludus Amphitheatre

medicus/medici Medical orderly

medicus ordinarius/medici ordinarii Doctor

mensor/mensores Surveyor

miles/milites Soldier

mille passus/milia passuum 'One-thousand paces' (Roman mile equal to 1,618 yards/1.48km)

milliaria/milliariae 'One-thousand strong'

missio causaria Medical discharge

missio ignominiosa Dishonourable discharge

modius/modii Unit-measure (equal to 8.62 litres)

murus caespiticius Turf wall

numerus/numeri 'Number' i.e. irregular infantry unit

optio/optiones *Centuria* second-in-command

pala/palae Spade

palus/pali Post for practising swordplay

papilio/papiliones Tent

panis militaris Army bread

passus/passus 'One-pace' (5 Roman feet equal to 4ft 10¼ inches/1.48m)

patera/paterae Mess-tin

pedes/pedites Infantryman

pereginus/peregini Non-Roman citizen

pes/pedes Roman foot (= 11½ inches/29.59cm)

phalera/phalerae Disc – military decoration

pila muralia Palisade stakes – double-pointed with central 'handgrip' to facilitate lashing

praefectus castrorum legionis *Legio* third-in-command responsible for logistics

praetentura Forward part of fort from *via principalis* to front gate (*porta praetoria*)

praetorium Commander's quarters

prandium Lunch

principales Three subordinate officers of a *centuria* (*optio, signifer, tesserarius*)

principia Headquarters

prosecutio Escort duty

quingenaria/quingenariae 'Five-hundred strong'

retentura Rear part of fort from *via quintana* to rear gate (*porta decumana*)

rutrum/rutri Shovel

sacramentum Oath of loyalty

sagittarius/sagittarii Archer

sesquiplicarius 1. *Turma* third-in-command 2. Pay-and-a-half

sestertius/sestertii Brass coin (equal to ¼ *denarius*)

sextarius/sextarii Unit-measure (equal to ¹⁄₁₆ *modius*)

signaculum/signacula Identity disc ('dog tag')

signifer Bearer of a standard of a *centuria* or *turma* – responsible for unit's finances

signum/signi 1. Standard 2. Watchword

stabulum/stabuli Stable-block

stipendium Pay

tabularium/tabularii Record-office

tessera/tesserae Plaque bearing password

tesserarius/tesserarii *Centuria* third-in-command – responsible for sentries and work parties

tiro/tirones Recruit

titulus/tituli Short mound with ditch forward of a gateway

torque/torques Neckband – military decorations

tres militiae Equestrian career-structure (*praefectus cohortis – tribunus angusticlavius – praefectus alae*)

tribunus/tribuni One of six senior officers, after the *legatus*, of a *legio*

tribunus militum legionis laticlavius: second-in-command (senatorial rank)

tribuni militum angusticlavii: five in total (equestrian rank)

tubicen/tubicenes Musician who blew the *tuba*, a trumpet used to signal commander's orders

turma/turmae *Ala* sub-unit

vallum Palisade

valetudinarium/valetudinaria Hospital

vexillarius/vexillarii Bearer of a *vexillum*

vexillatio/vexillationes Detachment

vexillum Standard of a *vexillatio*

via praetoria Road leading from *principia* to *porta praetoria*

via principalis Principle road extending across width of fort, from *porta principalis dextra* to *porta principalis sinistra*

via quintana Secondary road parallel to *via principalis*

via sagularis Perimeter road around *intervallum*

vicus/vici Extramural settlement (fort)

vitis Centurion's twisted-vine stick

Index

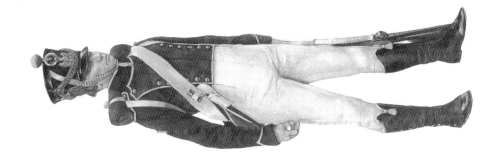

OSPREY PUBLISHING

FIND OUT MORE ABOUT OSPREY

❏ Please send me the latest listing of Osprey's publications

❏ I would like to subscribe to Osprey's e-mail newsletter

Title/rank

Name

Address

Postcode/zip   state/country

e-mail

I am interested in:

❏ Ancient world
❏ Medieval world
❏ 16th century
❏ 17th century
❏ 18th century
❏ Napoleonic
❏ 19th century

❏ American Civil War
❏ World War I
❏ World War II
❏ Modern warfare
❏ Military aviation
❏ Naval warfare

Please send to:

USA & Canada:
Osprey Direct USA, c/o MBI Publishing, P.O. Box 1,
729 Prospect Avenue, Osceola, WI 54020

UK, Europe and rest of world:
Osprey Direct UK, P.O. Box 140, Wellingborough,
Northants, NN8 2FA, United Kingdom

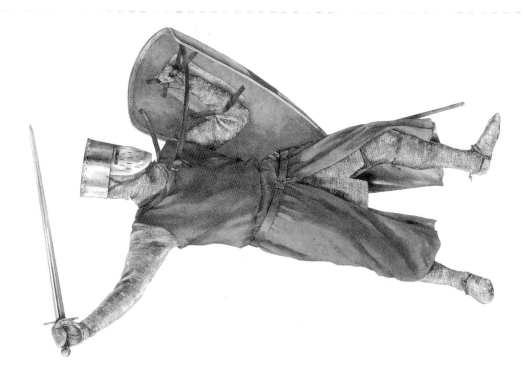

OSPREY
PUBLISHING

www.ospreypublishing.com

call our telephone hotline
for a free information pack

USA & Canada: 1-800-826-6600
UK, Europe and rest of world call:
+44 (0) 1933 443 863

Young Guardsman
Figure taken from Warrior 22:
Imperial Guardsman 1799–1815
Published by Osprey
Illustrated by Christa Hook

Knight, c.1190
Figure taken from *Warrior 1: Norman Knight 950 – 1204 AD*
Published by Osprey
Illustrated by Christa Hook

POSTCARD